BEHIND BARS

SURVIVING PRISON

BEHIND BARS

SURVIVING PRISON

JEFFREY IAN ROSS

STEPHEN C. RICHARDS

ALPHA

A Pearson Education Company

Dedicated to the men and women, both convicts and correctional officers, who on a daily basis survive the insanity behind bars.

International Standard Book Number: 0-02-864351-8
Library of Congress Catalog Card Number: 2002103794

04   03   02   8   7   6   5   4   3   2   1

Interpretation of the printing code: The rightmost number of the first series of numbers is the year of the book's printing; the rightmost number of the second series of numbers is the number of the book's printing. For example, a printing code of 02-1 shows that the first printing occurred in 2002.

Printed in the United States of America

Note: This publication contains the opinions and ideas of its authors. It is intended to provide helpful and informative material on the subject matter covered. It is sold with the understanding that the authors and publisher are not engaged in rendering professional services in the book. If the reader requires personal assistance or advice, a competent professional should be consulted.

For Marketing and Publicity, call (317) 581-3722

The publisher offers discounts on this book when ordered in quantity for bulk purchases and special sales.

For sales within the United States, please contact: Corporate and Government Sales, 1-800-382-3419 or corpsales@pearsontechgroup.com

Outside the United States, please contact: International Sales, (317) 581-3793 or international@pearsontechgroup.com

Publisher: Marie Butler-Knight

Product Manager: Phil Kitchel

Managing Editor: Jennifer Chisholm

Acquisitions Editor: Gary Goldstein

Development Editor: Jennifer Moore

Production Editor: Billy Fields

Copy Editor: Drew Patty

Cover/Book Designer: Trina Wurst

Creative Director: Robin Lasek

Indexer: Angie Bess

Proofreading: John Etchison, Elizabeth Louden

Layout: Angela Calvert

Crime is aggressive. So is the law.

—*from the motion picture* The Line-up, *Columbia, 1958,
directed by Don Siegel*

Contents

Introduction

Have you ever wondered what it's like to be in prison? Once incarcerated in a maximum, medium, or even minimum security prison, you lose most of your rights, all of your freedom, and a good dose of your self-esteem. We wrote this book as a no-nonsense explanation of prison life—for people who are simply curious about it as well as for those who have found themselves or loved ones in the unenviable position of serving a stiff stint in the joint.

Don't expect us to paint a pretty picture. Prison bears little resemblance to what you've seen in movies or read about in books. There's very little, if anything, about life in prison that's pleasing or fun. Unfortunately, an increasing number of Americans—and foreigners who are caught committing crimes on American soil—are learning about life on the inside the hard way: They're experiencing it. It only makes sense that the rest of us should know what it's like.

Most books about prison are written by academic criminologists, who know little about prisons because they have no firsthand experience and simply parrot outdated correctional theories and so-called empirical evidence they learned from other sheltered scholars. Most of these university "experts" have spent precious little time inside of penitentiaries or talking with convicts. If they were left unescorted in a penitentiary cellblock for ten minutes, they would probably have a heart attack.

If you want to know how the criminal justice and penal machinery functions, then ask a convict. They are the real authorities on prison conditions. *Behind Bars* is written by two veteran criminologists who have published extensively on crime and prisons. We have the experience to back up what we write: Ross worked almost four years inside a correctional institution, and Richards is an ex-convict, who spent eleven years in jail, prison, and on parole, including federal penitentiaries.

We tell it like it is, the "low-down and dirty" of what a person can expect if they go to jail or prison. Most of our information comes from firsthand experience or from conversations with convicts. Some in the legal world might call it hearsay, but for millions of prisoners behind bars in this country, it's a brutal reality. American convicts are subjected to degradations that few individuals on the outside want to know about—and would have trouble comprehending if they did.

You'll find answers to questions frequently asked by first-time convicts, such as "Will I be assaulted or raped in the first 24 hours on the inside? (Maybe, so be ready to defend yourself.) What will happen to my family and friends once I am incarcerated? (If it's a long sentence, there's a good chance they'll move on with their lives and forget about you.) What are the long-term effects of being in prison? (Depends on the individual, but statistics aren't very encouraging.) Will I be able to secure a good job after I am released? (Your chances are better if you get, or at least start working on, a college degree.)

Along the way we offer many tips for surviving the criminal justice system—from how to act if you're arrested to how to go about buying supplies from the prison commissary. Our aim in offering this advice is to help you make the best out of a really bad situation. The good news is, because you're reading this book, you're already following our first rule of prison survival: *Don't make the mistake of thinking that going to jail is something that only happens to other people.*

It could happen to you, if only because of bad timing or bad luck. Because you're reading this book, you're arming yourself with crucial information that everyone needs to know, the so-called law-abiding citizen most of all. Career criminals and jailhouse habitués already know it. And you need to know it *before* you're arrested, not after. After you're arrested it will be too late, because once those cold steel cuffs are clenching your wrists, the journey to prison may have already begun, and even one small misstep can have profound consequences.

Before starting on the hellish journey from arrest, through prosecution, to serving hard time, let's take a quick look at how many people are behind bars in Prison World, USA.

The Numbers Behind the Bars

The number of people being incarcerated at state and federal facilities continues to grow at an alarming rate. The most recent official estimate of persons in correctional custody, serving time in jail, prison, or on probation or parole is 6.47 million, with 3.8 million on probation and 725,527 on parole (Bureau of Justice Statistics, 2001). This total has tripled since 1980. These figures demonstrate that 1 in 32 Americans is under the control of the criminal justice system. This growth in the prison population is responsible for the largest prison construction boom in U.S. history. It means opening four new penitentiaries or correctional institutions every month.

But this estimate seriously underreports the total population in state and federal custody, in part because the numbers are growing so fast it's impossible to keep up with them, but also because the Bureau of Justice Statistics fails to count significant numbers of persons. Government statistics only total the numbers of persons in the "hard machine" (official custody of jails, prisons, probation, and parole).

These jail figures don't include the millions of people arrested and released every year without being formally charged. Recent estimates (U.S. Department of Justice) suggest that the 300,000 jail-day population, like inventory in a retail operation, turns over once every five days. This means that nearly 23 million people are locked up in local jails in the course of a year, with the same persons (e.g., homeless, derelicts, addicts, etc.) jailed numerous times. The more than 5 million people in correctional custody does not include juveniles, military prisoners, and mental patients.

Also neglected from the Bureau of Prison Statistics estimates are the tens of thousands of men, women, and children incarcerated by the U.S. Immigration and Naturalization Service (INS) in detention centers in El Paso, Laredo, and Port Isabel, Texas; Oakdale, Louisiana; El Centro, California; and Florence, Arkansas. Many of these tent prisons, called service and processing centers by the INS, have emergency capacities of 10,000 prisoners. Prisoners drop out of the official prison census when moved from jails or prisons to INS detention centers.

And with the stepped-up INS enforcement in the wake of the September 11, 2001, terrorist attacks, we can confidently expect a dramatic increase in the number of aliens arrested and incarcerated all over the country.

Confused Yet?

Corrections can be broken into two major categories, institutional and community. We are all familiar with institutional corrections: It encompasses the concrete and metal structures—the jails, prisons, and camps. In the shadow of these institutional structures is the world of community corrections, which includes all people on probation, on parole, and in halfway houses.

Within these two levels is a corrections system so complex as to confuse even the most astute of criminologists. People convicted of crimes can be sentenced to juvenile justice programs such as diversion, probation, and reform schools. They can be sentenced to participate in substance abuse programs, jails, and prisons. Probation may be granted as an alternative to incarceration, as a split sentence (prison, then probation), or as a second sentence to be served after prison. Parole, which refers to post-prison custody, can include lifetime parole, intensive supervision, and special parole (in which parolees can be returned to prison without credit for street time). And many prisoners are now serving split sentences, where they first serve prison time, then a second sentence of "community supervision" on top of that.

Meet Joe (and Jill) Convict

Contrary to popular belief, most people in jail and prison are not your typical "career criminals," such as bank robbers, counterfeiters, and mafia hit men. Instead, the vast majority of the prison population is made up of young, nonviolent, and first-time offenders. Over 90 percent of prisoners are male. About half of all prisoners are African-American, 20 percent Hispanic, and the rest mostly English-speaking Caucasians. Additionally, there is a growing number of special-needs prisoners (mentally ill and mentally retarded) serving time in prisons and community corrections facilities who are controlled with medication. Many of these individuals have slipped through the cracks of homeless shelters and community care centers to end up behind bars.

What Gives?

So why is this all taking place? In no small part because of the draconian drug laws that have been passed over the last two decades. The so-called "war on drugs" has dramatically increased a person's chance of being arrested, and decreased his or her ability to defend him or herself in court. (For instance, if your home is searched and a small amount of illegal drugs is found in your teenager's bedroom, you can be charged with conspiracy. The courts can use the threat of a conspiracy conviction to force you to either claim the illegal substance as your own or testify against your own child.)

Additionally, a number of changes have taken place in the states and at the federal level with respect to sentencing. These include truth in sentencing, the abolishment of parole, the eschewing of indeterminate sentencing, the notorious "three strikes and you're out" law, and mandatory minimums. These changes have had the net effect of increasing a person's chance of going to jail or prison ... and staying there. Determinate sentencing, with no parole, has resulted in tens of thousands of men and women, convicted of nonviolent offenses, being forced to serve decades in penitentiaries and correctional institutions. These men and women are growing impatient, and tension is building inside the fences and behind the walls.

Check, Please ...

Corrections is a big-money enterprise. It employs over 400,000 people, including administrators, corrections officers, psychologists, counselors, and social workers. And it's not just the federal and state governments running the show. Private for-profit companies such as Wackenhut and Corrections Corporation of America and not-for-profit organizations like the Salvation Army are also in the business of running correctional facilities.

Corrections costs taxpayers over $15 billion yearly. Although we can easily fix a dollar amount to this part of the American penal system, there are countless hidden costs, too, including loss of family income when a breadwinner is sentenced to prison, the increased possibility that a son or daughter of a convicted felon will follow in Daddy's—or Mommy's—felony footsteps, and the ugly shadow that the bulging corrections systems casts over the American landscape.

Before You Begin

One final word of caution. Because the information presented in this book is based on firsthand experience, the experiences of others, and extensive research we have conducted, what we say might not apply to every prisoner in every prison in the United States. Women, in particular, have a slightly different prison experience (see Chapter 11, "We Ain't No Debutantes: Women Behind Bars"). Still, this book is written by two "politically conscious" males and directed mostly toward men who face prison time. Our aim wasn't to present the universal prison experience, but to give you the information you need to survive a subterranean zone of "cons" patrolled by "hacks" (correctional officers), and security perimeters defended by high walls, razor and concertina wire (rolls of barbed wire ten feet tall that encircle prisons), and gun towers.

Acknowledgments

This book, like our previous work, is a truly collaborative affair. As such we would like to thank our agent Jimmy Vines for negotiating the project, Gary Goldstein at Alpha books for adopting and shepherding this book, and Billy Fields, Jennifer Moore, and Drew Patty for production matters.

We would also like to thank our students for enduring parts of this manuscript as lectures, and to our Convict Criminology colleagues, especially Richard S. Jones and Daniel S. Murphy, for comments.

Finally, we would like to extend our appreciation to our immediate families who have always been there in times of joy and crisis. Jeff wants to thank Natasha, Keanu, and Dakota; and Steve wants to thank Donna, Andre, Jan, and Brian.

Part 1

You're Under Arrest

Chapter 1

Busted!

America is a nation of laws that reach into every aspect of public and private life. By just going about the daily routine of trying to make a living, you run the risk of transgressing one or more strands of this invisible web of legal strictures and restraints.

An ordinary traffic stop by the police for something like a defective taillight could lead to your arrest for some long-forgotten (by you, anyway) unpaid parking tickets; a case of mistaken identity could land you a night in the county slammer before everything is straightened out; and participating in any kind of organized protest puts you at great risk of running afoul of the law. And then there are more serious offenses that can lead to your arrest, like dealing in illegal drugs, armed robbery, or murder.

No matter what the reason is for the arrest—and no matter if you're innocent or guilty—being arrested is serious business. Knowing the terrain will help you maximize your options to make the best of a bad situation.

From the moment you're placed under arrest, you enter a different world, a country-within-a-country, where the normal rules of behavior and niceties of society no longer apply.

You're Under Arrest

You never plan on getting arrested, even when you are doing illegal things. You don't step out your front door in the morning thinking: "Well, today is the day I finally get busted." Typically, you are in the wrong place at the wrong time. Someone picks you out of a crowd, and tells the cops you did it, or it is a routine traffic stop, and next thing you know you feel the long arm of the law on your shoulder. Most people think they can talk their way out of an arrest. But once the handcuffs are on, you are on your way to jail.

Besides typical nonviolent arrests, law enforcement also uses conspiracy indictments, Burn Laws, complicated sting operations, aggressive take-down procedures, informants, and exorbitant bail to make arrests and get convictions.

Conspiracy Convictions

The war on drugs is being fought at the state and federal level, especially with conspiracy convictions. The courts use conspiracy laws, coupled with secret grand juries, to indict defendants for indiscriminate associations, thoughts, and alleged attempts to violate law.

Conspiracy is defined as discussing, overhearing, or having knowledge of a plan to violate the law. As you can see, this casts a wide net. It is not necessary for the prosecution to prove direct involvement or that a crime actually happened. A person may be indicted for simply "having knowledge" of another person's activities. In other words, the mere intention to commit a crime is a crime. A person can even be indicted for knowing about another individual's attempt to either purchase or sell controlled substances.

Because a state's criminal code may not require the actual possession or sale of drugs for conspiracy indictments, prosecutors can construct cases out of circumstance, association, and hearsay, and then invent their own sentencing guidelines based on imaginary quantities of controlled substances. Despite the lack of physical evidence in conspiracy cases, the arresting officers and court functionaries, working together, rarely lose a case.

Burn Laws

In some states, under what's called the "Burn Law," the police can even arrest a person for selling counterfeit illegal drugs. A common ploy of some police is to send an undercover officer into neighborhood taverns or hangouts to solicit drug buys. The cop will sit at the bar and flash $100 bills at the patrons, asking "Does anyone have coke for sale?"

Now, everyone in the bar knows the man is a narc. Still, there's always some slick dude who pours salt or sugar in a napkin, sells it to the officer, hoping to make a quick buck and getaway. All too predictably, the person is busted. The cops get a collar, some lawyer gets a fee, the district attorney gets another easy conviction, and the poor fool goes to jail.

Take Downs

These days, many arrests start with a take-down. Using what are sometimes called "No-Knock Warrants," local, state, or federal agents (and sometimes a combined force) armed with automatic weapons and shotguns may, without so much as a knock on the door or a ring of the doorbell, use a battering ram to smash your door off its hinges and enter your home or place of work.

Convicts will tell you about take-down procedures, search and destroy schemes, and early morning raids. It is not unusual to hear stories of large men representing a drug strike force wearing military dress, including flak vests and helmets, bursting into the homes, offices, and businesses of suspects.

Their uniforms often identify them as belonging to numerous law enforcement agencies: city, county, and state police departments; the Drug Enforcement Agency (DEA); the Federal Bureau of Investigation (FBI); the Immigration and Naturalization Service (INS); the Bureau of Alcohol, Tobacco, and Firearms (BATF); and Customs. During raids or arrests, dozens of backup officers often will surround the premises.

The government employs overwhelming force as a means to protect their own, to eliminate resistance, and to prevent the escape of suspects. The police push people to the floor, handcuff them, search for weapons, and then tear the premises apart looking for evidence. They may use hammers or crowbars to break televisions, punch holes in walls, or rip apart beds and furniture.

Unfortunately, drug raids do go awry. Incorrect addresses are entered, innocent people arrested, personal property destroyed in the search for evidence, and occasionally, people get injured, shot, or killed. Despite this activity, sometimes the officers do not have search or arrest warrants, seize materials beyond the scope of the warrant, and/or find no weapons or drugs. Such exercises may amount to little more than fishing expeditions or zealous forms of harassment.

What you may have seen of such raids on TV cop shows can be quite different from the real thing. The normal procedure goes like this:

The police stake out a house for a few days, using surveillance techniques and technologies to determine on what day and how to make the raid. Most often they will strike in the dead of night, when the occupants of the house are deemed to be most vulnerable. They may first neutralize the family dog, especially such formidable breeds as pit bulls, Rottweilers, or German shepherds. The animal can be taken out with drugged meat or tranquilizer darts. The watchdog down, the raiders then disable any potential getaway vehicles, usually by punching holes in the tires. They then strike with swift, devastating force, simultaneously crashing through front and back doors, sometimes coming in like modern day ninjas through the windows. You may be jolted from a sound sleep to find one of them pointing a shotgun or assault rifle in your face.

If you should be so unlucky as to be the object of such a raid, do not assume that the intruders will look like police, wearing blue uniforms and badges. They may seem like regular civilians, some even with long hair, dreadlocks, cornbraids, and beards. Should you mistake them for some local thugs trying to rip you off and try to defend yourself by reaching for a weapon stored in your night table, you may succeed in getting yourself and whomever shares your bed killed.

When the police come through the door, you *must* "freeze." Stand still with your hands in clear sight over your head. Let the police take you down to the floor and apply the handcuffs. Direct your family, including children, to do the same. If you have a large dog inside the house when the raiders strike, pray that things don't get messy.

Be warned: If you like to party, keep fast company, or live next door to a drug dealer (or even if you don't), it pays to be aware of your surroundings. Keep your eyes open and pay attention to un-usual events in your neighborhood. If you find your dog knocked out or dead in the backyard, a flat tire on your vehicle, or strange men parked in cars or vans on the street for long hours at a stretch, it may be time to take the wife and kids on that long-promised trip to Disneyland.

Sting Operations

One of law enforcement's more insidiously effective inventions is the strategy of coupling the "weak burden of proof" required by conspiracy laws with the bag of tricks and deceit used to work sting operations. Judges, prosecutors, and police design and employ stings to cast a wide net. The more defendants indicted, the easier it is to get a conviction by coercing one or more co-defendants to testify against the others.

A "sting" refers to undercover agents attempting to purchase drugs, weapons, stolen goods, or political influence. "Reverse stings," often used by federal authorities, involve agents posing as smugglers, distributors, or dealers, offering to sell drugs. These operations are particularly nebulous when pursued as conspiracy cases, which do not require the completion of a drug transaction. Authorities design a crime, a criminal scenario, and then entice people to participate in their trap. The agents are most successful when the activity is vague, ill-defined, and limited to casual conversation, as opposed to specific business arrangements, transactions, exchanges of product for cash, or deliveries of controlled substances. Criminal indictments are based on agreeing to participate in something that need not happen. In an admittedly extreme case, a federal agent can solicit a person to buy drugs in a crowded bar with loud music, and the victim, not understanding the offer, can simply nod his or her head and be arrested. No display or exchange of drugs for money is required. Of course, in some cases, a great defense lawyer has a chance of beating the rap in court.

We are not implying that all folks who are arrested are for the most part innocent, or that law enforcement is made up entirely of bad, lazy, evil people; but there is enough of this phenomena to make us wary of the criminal justice system.

Arrest and Aftermath

After having your hands cuffed behind your back and getting a thorough pat down, you will be given a ride in the back of a police car or van to the local lockup. Depending on which law enforcement agency made the arrest, you will either be transported to the nearby district or division police station; central booking, which is located in or near the municipal courthouse; the federal courthouse; or taken directly to the county jail.

You will soon discover whether you're charged with a misdemeanor or a felony. If that official piece of paper says it's a misdemeanor (less than a year in jail), the police think you've committed a relatively minor crime; if a felony (one year to life, or death), then you've got serious problems.

No matter where the police take you, the routine is basically the same. You will be booked, which means you will be strip-searched, fingerprinted, and photographed (also known as getting your official mug shot). Then you are placed in a holding cell. Alternatively, you may spend a couple of hours at the local police station, then be transported down to central booking, where you'll wait an hour or two before picture and print time. Lock up facilities vary in size and smell, usually with no bed and only a bench to sit on. Sometimes you are held in your own cell, with another person, or placed in what they call a "bullpen" or "drunk tank," with 50 or 100 other people.

The first thing you need to remember is *keep your mouth shut and do not discuss your arrest or case with anyone, police or fellow inmates.*

Jailhouse holding tanks are usually bugged with hidden microphones and video cameras. This technology is only incidentally for your protection. Its primary function is to provide the judicial system with an opportunity to gather more incriminating evidence.

Your jailers need not rely on sophisticated electronic surveillance, though, as a few of your cellmates may be more than happy to inform law enforcement of anything you say. These jailhouse snitches will convey your conversation to the police as a means, or so they hope, of reducing their own sentences or jail time. In a major case like homicide, rape, or large-scale drug conspiracy, you can be sure there will be an undercover cop in your cell, trying to position himself as your new "best friend."

All trips to prison begin with some jail time. This is usually, if computed properly, later deducted from prison "time to be served." Most prisoners consider city and county jails to be worse than prison, especially facilities in large cities and the deep South. Generally, jails have only holding cells, cellblocks with day rooms, and solitary confinement. Cells are crowded with bunk beds stacked two or three high, with a dozen or more men in each cage. These facilities have very little, if any, medical, recreational, or educational services. Other settings may be boot camp or dormitory style, with countless rows of cots and bunk beds.

Most local lock-up facilities are staffed by "turnkey" guards, who are paid close to minimum wage, and often come from a socio-economic background similar to that of most of the prisoners. (Except the turnkeys are outside the bars, looking in.) The lock-ups are sometimes jammed with men sleeping in the day rooms and on mattresses along the hallway floors. Filthy cells can be infested with lice, cockroaches, and even rodents. The sub-par food includes those jailhouse staples, bologna sandwiches and Kool-Aid.

One of the authors of this book remembers a jail in the deep South where every meal consisted of cornbread, grits, and coffee. In the evening, they would serve fish heads (complete with eyeballs and teeth) that were said to be donated by a nearby naval base. The stench would waft down the hall, preceding the dinner carts. Some of the guards would make their rounds late at night with a grocery cart, selling potato chips and candy bars.

In most big cities in the U.S., the jail population is largely black, Hispanic, and young. The cells may be filled with poor, illiterate juveniles possibly facing years in prison. Very few of these prisoners will have the nerve and financial resources to fight their cases. They plead guilty to get out of jail, to be released to the street for "time served," or to be moved to the state prison system.

Older and experienced cons may help the youngsters by interpreting their legal papers, preparing them for court, and "comforting" them after they plead guilty and return to the cellblocks with long sentences and tears running down their faces.

The Phone Call

When do you get your one phone call? Although you may have to wait a day or two, you'll eventually get it. When you do, be careful who you call and what you say. All jail phone calls are definitely recorded by the authorities, and the numbers that are dialed are handed over to the police. In order to secure additional incriminating evidence, the FBI or local police can simply pick up the taped conversations and phone numbers called.

For instance, if you call your drug connection or customers to warn them about what just transpired, the police will have your recorded conversation and your connections' names, addresses, and phone numbers.

Whomever you call, *never discuss your case on the phone.* Any admission of guilt will be used against you in court. Let us repeat: Any admission of guilt will be used against you in court.

The same warning applies to mail, both sent or received, which will be opened and copied by jail staff. Remember, *you have no privacy in jail,* and every word you say, phone call you make, or letter you write, can be used in court to make a case against you or drum up additional indictments against you or others.

Being a prisoner means having your time and space controlled by others. Even the stainless steel toilets are in plain sight.

Stay Focused

Up to now, especially if this is your first time behind bars, you'll be more or less in a state of shock. How the hell are you going to get out of this mess?

Now's the time to find out what you're made of. Being arrested may seem like the end of the world, but there's a lot you can do to help yourself if you keep a clear head and don't lose your nerve.

Never mind all those prison movies you've seen. This is the real thing. Figuring out the true from the false is vital, and operating on the basis of Hollywood myths and misconceptions is counterproductive at best and potentially dangerous. Like getting cancer, going to jail is one of those ultimate reality checks.

Begin by putting your financial and legal house in order. Make a mental (not written) inventory of your assets, both financial and psychological. Consider the worst-case options and plan accordingly. Do you have any dependents? Do you have a will? When was the last time it was updated? Do you have an accountant, do you need one? Who's going to protect your financial interests if you're sentenced to a long stretch in prison?

If you're employed or attend a school or university, you may want to invent a cover story to protect your reputation, or more importantly, to avoid being fired or kicked out of school. If not the truth, be prepared with a plausible explanation to account for the events and/or circumstances of your arrest. This is important if you need to demonstrate to a judge that you're an upstanding member of the community or if you have to pay legal expenses.

Then again, if the charges against you are serious or you are a well-known member of the community, it will probably be in the next day's newspaper or on nightly news, or the cops will pay your employer a visit. In which case, a cover story won't be much help.

Chapter 2

Four Fatal Legal Mistakes (and How to Avoid Them)

Most folks have no idea what to expect when arrested and charged with a criminal offense, and so they are often at a total loss as to how to handle the situation. When it comes to being arrested, ignorance *isn't* bliss. In the first few minutes or hours, before they are able to consult an attorney, people often make fatal mistakes that ultimately seal their fate.

Here are four common blunders that defendants need to avoid.

The Right to Remain Silent

The first fatal error many people make is talking to the police. You do not have to answer their questions. When you're arrested, *shut up.*

Don't be hostile or challenging about it, just don't say a thing. Talking to the cops is the last thing a defense lawyer wants his or her client to do, if the attorney is hoping to successfully beat the rap (more on lawyers later). No matter how nice or threatening the officers appear, it is wise not to say anything—not one word—to the police. Many people do not realize that if they talk to the cops, every word they say "can and will be used against" them. When they arrest you, you need to realize that the police are not your friends. They don't necessarily hate you, either. You are part of a job to them. If, after having been read your Miranda rights, you make statements that can be used to convict you, they will be used against you.

A suspect, defendant, or prisoner is protected from self-incrimination by *Gideon v. Wainwright,* 392 U.S. 335 (1963) and *Miranda v. Arizona,* 384 U.S. 436 (1966) (the right to counsel), which held that defendants have the right to protection from self-incrimination and are entitled to the assistance of a lawyer. This extends from federal to state law under the provisions of the 14th Amendment of the U.S. Constitution. (The Gideon decision was the basis of the book and movie *Gideon's Trumpet,* which showed how a poor, uneducated man—Henry Fonda in the screen adaptation—with only a legal pad and pencil could appeal to the U.S. Supreme Court and be provided with free legal counsel.)

The Miranda warning is read to all suspects when they are formally placed under arrest. The warning includes a statement such as, "You have the right to remain silent, if you talk to any police officer, anything you say can and will be used against you in court. You have the right to stop answering at any time. You have the right to an attorney. If you cannot afford a lawyer, one will be provided to you free of cost."

It's astounding how many individuals, after having been read their Miranda rights, will keep on talking, to their own detriment. Again—and we cannot stress this point too plainly—when you're arrested, *shut up.*

When, exactly, the Miranda warning is read varies from one arrest or jurisdiction to the next, but it occurs sometime between the time cuffs have been placed on you and you're cooling your heels in a holding cell.

Retaining an Attorney

The second error defendants make is paying their lawyer in advance. They learn this valuable lesson all too late when they run out of cash. While most criminal defense attorneys require a retainer, the client or their concerned friends and family should only offer a modest sum, a few thousand dollars. The fact is, lawyers are not shy about demanding money from new clients. Attorneys are expensive, and they expect to be paid. When they're not being paid, they're not your lawyers anymore. Nothing personal, it's just business.

Now for a lesson in the hard economic realities of crime and punishment. Until they've been arrested, most folks have no idea how expensive a criminal defense can be. A simple misdemeanor in a local court close to home may "only" cost a few thousand dollars. By comparison, a felony, especially if it's in an out-of-state jurisdiction, may require a few hundred thousand by the time it's all over.

Dealing with a lawyer is like riding in a taxi cab: The meter is always running. Attorneys charge anywhere from fifty to a few hundred dollars an hour, and bill the client for expenses, which may include long distance telephone calls, travel (including hotels and meals), filing fees, court transcripts, private investigators, expert witnesses, and legal staff. In a serious case, your lawyer may require the services of additional legal talent to prepare for court (paralegals, legal research staff, etc.), or a full-blown defense team for trial proceedings. If the case is in another state or federal court, where your lawyer has not been admitted to the bar, you may need to pay for local counsel—another attorney to represent you before the court.

Lawyer fees and travel expenses add up quickly. You may have to pay for airline tickets, rental cars, and hotel rooms for the attorney and his or her staff as they travel to and from court in various jurisdictions. And remember, lawyers rarely stay at budget motels and eat at fast-food restaurants. Each of the many court appearances (arraignment, preliminary, numerous pre-trial, bail revocation hearings, and trials) can cost thousands of dollars. Remember, part of the prosecution's strategy is to deplete the defendant's legal defense fund.

Most people simply don't have $10,000 or $20,000 lying around to pay for a lawyer. Unlike buying a car or home, rarely can legal expenses be paid in installments, or a few months after services are rendered, as in medical bills. Although some lawyers take credit cards, you will have to be creative in making suitable arrangements to pay for your defense.

In general, with few exceptions, attorneys want their money up front, in advance, or they leave you to throw yourself on the mercy of the court. The reasons are simple enough. If you are found guilty and sent to prison, you will be in no mood to pay your legal bill. Also, many of their clients are crooks who are not overly inclined toward scrupulous bill-paying in the first place. These facts lawyers know only too well, so they will exert great pressure on you to pay up front before your case is decided. You must resist their demands for large sums of money and only pay the attorney a portion of what they ask.

Defense attorneys are like stockbrokers: They collect their fees and commissions on the amount of business they do, no matter whether their customers win or lose. As officers of the court, their first allegiance is to the legal system, even at the expense of their clients. Most lawyers who practice in criminal courts make a good living losing most of their cases, a fact that they rarely share with their clients.

The vast majority of people arrested on serious charges have no money to retain quality legal representation. They can't afford the services of an experienced private trial lawyer, so they either hire some youngster fresh out of law school or are represented by a court-appointed public defender. Public defenders generally are sincere and concerned individuals, overworked, underpaid, and usually unable to give each case the attention it requires.

When it comes to attorneys, remember to watch your wallet. Always demand an itemized written bill for services, negotiate the bottom line, and never pay them all of what they want up front. Despite their smiles and reassurances like "don't worry about anything," when you run out of cash the lawyer will run out on you.

Bail and Bond

Most people don't understand the difference between bail and bond and how they work. Apart from the discomfiture of being in jail, it's doubly difficult to try to fight a case from inside a cell. Bail is usually set by a judge, magistrate, or commissioner at the arraignment hearing, which is your first appearance in court.

Typically, in serious cases, bail may range from a few thousand to a million dollars or more. The defendant somehow must arrange for family or friends to come up with this sum to effect their release from jail or a holding facility. Bail provides the court a guarantee that the defendant will appear in court for their next scheduled hearing and will not disappear. In most jurisdictions, bail must be provided in full.

In comparison, bond is some percentage of bail. For example, if bail is $10,000, the defendant might be allowed by the court (this depends on the jurisdiction) to pay a 10 percent fee ($1,000) and provide collateral (car or home) to a bonding company (usually right down the street from the courthouse), which then posts the full amount with the court. In this situation, the defendant forfeits the $1,000 even if the case is dismissed or the trial ends in an acquittal. If the defendant fails to appear in court, or jumps bail by running from the law, the bail bond company is required to cover the $10,000 with the court. Bonding companies are not in business to lose money and will send armed, licensed operatives to apprehend the fugitive and return him or her to custody.

An alternative to spending 10 percent at a bonding company, is to post a surety bond. This is a lien on property—usually a home, business, auto, or financial investment (certificate of deposit, money market account, or mutual fund)—where equity is established and accounts are verified. This is what people mean when they say they put up their house or car for a relative or friend.

Your attorney will charge a fee for making the proper arrangements, drawing up the papers, and presenting the documentation to the court. The liens are released after the case is settled, either by acquittal or conviction, or bail is revoked and you are jailed as the criminal case continues in court. Your lawyer will bill you again to petition the court to lift the liens, clear your credit, and return your property. The advantage to this procedure is that you, family, or friends can post your bail without liquidating assets. The disadvantage is that the arrangements require more lawyer time and fees, and if you fail to appear in court, you or your benefactors may lose their property.

Exorbitant bail is a tool used by prosecutors to force defendant cooperation. After being arrested and jailed, persons go to court where the bail may be intentionally set in excess of what the defendant can reasonably be expected to afford, depending upon the lack of "cooperation."

Many persons indicted on criminal charges give oral or written statements, what are called confessions, as a means to get out of jail, because they cannot raise bail. Some plead "nolo contendere" (no contest). Others take an Alford plea, in which they don't actually admit wrongdoing, but recognize that prosecutors have enough evidence to convict them. Still, many so-called "friendly defendants," who have already established their role as informants (or those who will), walk out on personal recognizance (a promise to reappear at a later date). Uncooperative defendants, however, may spend many months, even years, awaiting trial, if they are unable to raise bail or the courts deem them too dangerous or too much of a flight-risk to release on bail. Most people arrested on serious felony charges do not get out of jail on bail.

Depending on the jurisdiction, most misdemeanors can be settled (i.e., conviction or dismissal) relatively quickly by paying a fine or spending a few months in jail. Fighting a serious felony indictment can take many months or even years, especially if it involves a jury trial and stretches into appellate review (in which the original verdict of a trial is appealed to a higher-level court). Meanwhile, your family is scared to death, employers are looking to replace you, lawyers demand more money, and your spouse begins weighing the relative merits of your eventual demise and absence. They are all waiting for the other shoe to drop or the axe to fall, and some (if not all of them) may be getting impatient.

If you get lucky and are able to post bail, bond, or be released on your own recognizance, you will enter that nether world of pretrial supervision. This may include both jail time that does count and community bail supervision that does not count toward the completion of an anticipated criminal sentence.

Bail: Living in Limbo

Prisoners released on bail may be ordered by courts to report to probation or parole offices, or pretrial service agencies on a daily or weekly basis for months or years while they await the disposition of their criminal cases. This may be as simple as a phone call or as tiresome as making a personal appearance once a day, being subjected to a urine test, and wearing an ankle bracelet (electronic monitoring device). These defendants are subject to the same rules and restrictions as probationers and parolees, including travel prohibitions, searches of their home, and restrictions on association with certain persons in the community.

Being on bail can be an existential experience, like you're a walking ghost of the living dead, attending your own funeral. It can be surreal listening to friends and relatives make future plans without you, dividing up the spoils (if any will be left after your defense), as if you were already dead and buried. They may discuss your eventual leaving in your presence, as if you are not in the room. Even if they love you and believe in your innocence, they may have little faith in the courts, your legal defense, or future trial deliberations. They might talk openly about this, and even blame you for all the headaches and confusion resulting from your problem. And they're right—ultimately it's your problem, not theirs.

You never know who your friends are, or for that matter your loved ones, until you've "caught a criminal charge." The process of discovering this may not be pleasant. If you're convicted of a serious crime and sentenced to prison, all your worldly assets and roles will be up for grabs. You may or may not need them. In any case, the longer you are locked up, the more likely your possessions will disappear and roles diminish.

Your business partners may welcome your departure and try to claim your share of the company. If you're professionally employed, one of your former colleagues or subordinates may get your job. Your teenager is already washing your car and asking for the keys. Your former friends may start hitting on your wife. And your loving spouse is probably already contemplating the cold place you'll leave in the bed—and how to fill it. When a spouse goes to jail, the other often files for divorce and full custody of the children.

Love fades and life goes on, with or without you. Your family will survive your departure, maybe even better than you dare imagine. After all, most people welcome receiving inherited assets. Your going to prison is like a death in the family, minus the medical bills, bedside vigil, or funeral expenses. If they care, the others can write or come to visit you in the pen. But the longer you stay incarcerated, the more you lose. Stay in prison long enough and even the most loving of families are liable to forget you ever existed.

Due Process and Let's Make a Deal

You may think the 14th Amendment guarantees you due process, meaning bail, attorney, and a trial by peers. Unfortunately, after being locked up in the county jail, you discover that bail may be denied, lawyers are expensive, and few defendants ever get a trial. The fact is, most people plead guilty to a lesser or reduced charge simply because they get tired of being locked up in jail, their legal defense funds run out, and they fear the possible consequences of losing a trial.

These are the cold, hard equations of crime and punishment. Most cases never go to trial. The attorney persuades the defendant (often after the lawyer has bled the patient dry of money for pre-trial hearings) not go to trial, arguing that if they lose—and they probably will—they will be sentenced to the full extent of the law.

Yes, you have a Constitutional right to a fair trial, but if you exercise that right and lose the case, the prosecution most likely will demand severe sentencing penalties, in return for your having made them take the case to trial. Fight them and lose, and they'll up the ante on the penalties. So the lawyer tells you to admit your guilt and the prosecutor will either reduce charges or ask the judge to limit the sentence.

And don't delude yourself into thinking that the "Speedy Trial Act" will shorten your time doing pre-trial detention in the local jail. Under federal law, this piece of legislation (passed in 1974) provides that, once arrested or detained, a defendant is entitled to a court hearing within 100 days. This does not mean a bench (judge only) or jury trial. Instead, it simply means that while you are in jail or on bail, the court must schedule an *appearance* every 100 days. These appearances can be pre-trial hearings, bail revocation proceedings and the like, and they are perfect opportunities for your lawyer to send you another bill.

The Lowdown on Snitches

"Informants," the police call them. Others refer to them as "rats," "snitches," or even nastier names. These "cooperating individuals" will name and denounce acquaintances and associates as participants in alleged conspiracies. They may be recruited by the police and paid in money, (or, it's rumored, secretly with narcotics), or reduction of charges in exchange for their cooperation. Prosecutors and police officers put on the pressure by threatening the accused with multiple counts, indictment of friends and family members, and possible life sentences.

You might think you'd never snitch on your friends or acquaintances or plead guilty to a crime, but you might end up singing like a bird once the cops and prosecutors are through with you. Law enforcement agents may threaten to arrest your family, terminate parental rights, confiscate assets, and audit several years' worth of bank account statements or personal or business tax returns, to compel confessions, collaborating testimony, and plea bargains.

They employ the "mathematics of terror," underscoring the maximum number of months you may spend in custody, to bully you into pleading guilty and/or becoming an informer. And don't make the mistake of thinking that you'll only have to serve a small percentage of your sentence. Under federal law, all prisoners, even snitches, have no possibility of parole (released from prison, but still under the supervision of the courts) and must do at least 85 percent of their legal commitment. In comparison, most states still allow the possibility of parole. State prisoners where parole is still an option may be released from prison after serving, for example, one fourth or third of court ordered time.

Many indicted suspects are so intimidated by the possibility of being sentenced to decades in prison that they plead guilty, sometimes making up stories about friends or even strangers, as a means to reduce their own sentence. One may see co-conspirators recite prepared or rehearsed statements on the witness stand, and if they hesitate or deviate from the script, are threatened again with the withdrawal of their plea bargain. Defense objections that government witnesses have extensive criminal convictions, or that testimony is coerced and paid for with a reduced sentence or money, are often overruled by unsympathetic judges.

The name of the prosecutorial game is pressure. Law enforcement personnel have no need to physically torture defendants—not when psychological stress is so effective. They compel confessions, and use collaborating testimony and plea bargains. Unabashedly, they seek to break the will of the defendants, "rolling them over" and "turning" them into government witnesses.

Despite their openly avowed detestation of informers, rare indeed are the professional criminals who have not at some time in their careers made a deal with police to inform on others to win some benefit for themselves. Omerta (the code of silence) and the fearsome measures taken to enforce it have not kept even top Mafiosi from going to prison, thanks to the testimony of their brothers in crime.

A note of warning: Defendants who cut deals with prosecutors can easily be identified, as the case may appear in the press and the court papers are public record. Once in prison, this information may be used by other prisoners to label the person an informer, giving them a "snitch jacket." Thus their time in jail will suddenly become more difficult, or even lead to a quick shank (prison knife) in the ribs.

Stand Up and Plead, "Not Guilty, Your Honor"

The most common mistake made by defendants is not knowing when to stand and make a fight of it. There are a number of advantages to pleading not guilty, being what is known as a "stand-up guy" and fighting your case all the way through a full-blown trial, either by judge or jury.

Remember, you have the right to remain silent (Miranda rights), backed up and guaranteed by the famous U.S. Supreme Court decision, but only if you continue to plead innocent. Once you decide to bargain, unless you can arrange an Alford plea or nolo contendere (no contest), which may not be allowed by the judge or prosecution, you will be forced to plea bargain, which means confess to a crime.

This may have serious and even dangerous future consequences. For example, your plea bargain and confession may not be accepted unless it implicates other people and leads to their indictments, and it may require your court testimony. At best, you get a reduced charge, burning bridges along the way. At worst, this could get you killed.

Another possibility, rarely understood by first-time defendants, but well known to those with lengthier police records, is that once you plead guilty, which becomes public record and part of your police criminal justice dossier, you are more likely to be rearrested, and are easier to convict.

Consider this scenario: The police arrest two people in a car with one bag of marijuana. The first person has a prior conviction in which they confessed, while the second has a similar outcome, but fought the case through jury trial and appeals. Who do you think the prosecutors will charge with possession of the pot?

Easy: the person who previously told the truth and cooperated with the authorities. He saves the court time and the messy details and costs of a trial. Those who fold will be charged every time. Cops, prosecutors, and judges prefer to avoid scheduling another trial, as this requires their time and public funds.

By contrast, the second person has already proven himself a stand-up guy, who upon being arrested keeps his or her mouth shut, does not confess or give statements against others, pleads not guilty, demands a trial, and refuses to cooperate with prosecutors.

Remember, a defense attorney best represents a client in a trial if the defendant retains his or her right to remain silent. This stubborn individual will keep his or her mouth shut, and demand due process as guaranteed by the 14th Amendment (a trial with all the trimmings), and if his or her luck improves, may be released. The case gets old after all those pre-trial hearings three months apart. Maybe the evidence mistakenly disappears or gets lost, the witnesses lose their memory or maybe even disappear, the arresting officer is convicted of police brutality or retires from the force.

This is especially likely after the authorities pin the rap on our first defendant, who was so willing to confess his sins. The police might not care who the drugs belong to; their concern is to secure an easy conviction that clears the books, which means charge the first person, who already has a history of folding under pressure.

The last individual they want to prosecute is the stand-up guy who will make them prove their case at trial. That's too much work for a system that is used to easy pickings. By comparison, he who pleads guilty seals his own fate when he confesses. He gets no trial, only the belated and dismaying realization that, by "pleading out," he has "rolled" on himself.

Make no mistake: The person who is considering demanding due process needs to be tough, as the courts can come down hard on those who refuse to deal away their rights. It may be argued that quite often, the courts' day-to-day participation in the war on crime compromises its claim to impartiality. They punish defendants who exercise their Constitutional rights to due process (14th Amendment): right to remain silent, bail, an attorney, jury of your peers, and appeal. These "non-cooperative conspirators" may be subject to aggressive prosecution, which includes confiscation of assets, trial by press, intimidation of legal representation and family, and being threatened with multiple indictments. They may spend months or years in county jail, as the court and defense attorney delay proceedings through numerous pre-trial hearings.

After the defendant is convicted, the judge orders the probation or parole office to conduct a Pre-Sentence Investigation (PSI), which is similar to a police interrogation. This is one more opportunity for law enforcement to gather information about you. A probation/parole officer will write up a thorough report detailing your education, employment, family, bad habits, and degree of cooperation. Then the trial judge will use this document to inform his or her decision at sentencing. If the defendant refuses to cooperate with the PSI, the officer may resort to intimidation and threats of bail revocation. As the months pass and the defendant proceeds through trial and appeals, his or her phones may be tapped, mail monitored, house kept under surveillance, and relatives, friends, and neighbors questioned. No matter how much they try to coerce you, you are not legally required to help the probation/parole authorities write a PSI.

Some say that despite the pressure and risks, it may be better to keep your mouth shut, retain your right to remain silent, refuse to plea bargain, and take your chances with a jury trial. This keeps you from having to inform on your friends, allowing you to retain some measure of self-respect as you begin your prison sentence. You may even have a better chance of surviving prison with your dignity and life intact. Besides, most defendants who plead guilty get only a token reduction in penalty, still go to prison, and may do almost as much time as those convicted at trial. The bottom line is to make the authorities prove it in court.

So there you have it. A misdemeanor arrest will cost you time and money. Arrest and conviction on a serious charge may cost you your business, family, and friends. Fight the charge and lose, and be more severely punished for making the prosecution fight its case. Fight the charge and win, and it'll still cost you a fortune in lawyer's fees. Nice, eh?

Part 2

You've Got Jail!

Chapter 3

Big Houses, Dog Pens, and Gladiator Schools: The U.S. Prison System

The dramatic increase in the numbers of Americans incarcerated has created a boom in prison construction. Hundreds of new prisons have been and are being built. These correctional facilities, both urban and rural, range from minimum to super maximum security. Prisons are run by states and the federal government, and there are even a few private correctional facilities.

Doing State Time

State prisons are answerable to the state commissioner or director of corrections, who is appointed by the governor. He or she has the power to appoint wardens, who are responsible for the day-to-day operation of their individual correctional facilities. State convicts are convicted of crimes particular to each individual state and criminal codes vary from state to state as do penalties for certain offences. For example, in California, all things being equal, a first-time conviction for possession of four ounces of marijuana may lead to a fine and probation; in Texas, this may lead to some jail time.

State prisons have large numbers of individuals coming from impoverished backgrounds and neighborhoods. In many states with large urban areas, the prisons will have a large African-American population. In California, Texas, and the Southwest, it might help to know some Spanish. Do time in Kentucky, West Virginia, or Tennessee, and you will meet lots of folks from economically depressed Appalachia, convicted of armed robbery, auto theft, and selling moonshine. Alaska prisons might feature Native Americans and Inuit for violating game and fishing regulations, or oil pipeline workers picked up in barroom brawls. The kind of time you do depends on where it is you're doing it.

The number of prisoners varies from state to state, with states like California, Georgia, Texas, and South Carolina having higher incarceration rates per capita than any other states in the union. States like Vermont and Minnesota, however, pride themselves on keeping offenders out of institutions.

Doing Federal Time

Some convicts take a kind of perverse pride in being prisoners of the U.S. government. Federal prisoners are considered the elite of the prison world. These are the men and women who local authorities were unable to corner, arrest, and convict. Some of them actually beat state charges with high-powered lawyers, but were then reindicted under federal law (this is called federal oversight). Others were simply too quick, savage, or sophisticated for city, county, or state police agencies.

The Federal Bureau of Prisons (FBOP) is thought by convicts to operate a better system than most states. The prisons are cleaner, with more desirable food, and the prison staff is better educated, trained, and paid. It is fair to say that most prisoners would prefer to do federal time, day for day, as compared to state time.

That said, federal prisoners are usually allowed fewer material possessions than state convicts. Individuals serving time in state prisons may have their own televisions, collections of books, music, clothes, and posters or pictures hung on their cell walls. Federal prison cells are more austere. These prisoners are restricted to only basic items, such as five books, toiletries, a few changes of institutional clothes, no television. All of these possessions must be able to fit in one small locker.

Federal prisoners usually do more time than state prisoners, too. The federal sentencing guidelines often punish nonviolent offenders more harshly than those convicted of violent offenses. Under federal law, a person may be sentenced to more prison time for growing or distributing marijuana or selling cocaine than for bank robbery or murder. FBOP cellblocks are filled with prisoners doing life sentences for drug convictions, with no possibility of parole. It is not uncommon to hear federal prison staff comment on the insanity of drug war sentences.

The FBOP operates prisons all over the country, institutions identified by their acronyms, including Administrative Detention Maximums (ADX), United States Penitentiaries (USP), Federal Correctional Institutions (FCI), Federal Prison Camps (FPC), Federal Medical Centers (FMC), Federal Detention Centers (FDC), Metropolitan Correctional Centers (MCC), and Federal Transport Centers (FTC).

In the federal correctional system there are no states, only six FBOP administrative districts: North East, Mid-Atlantic, South East, North Central, South Central, and West. This is a prison system that has officially repudiated rehabilitation, has the longest sentences in the world, and no parole (for persons convicted since 1987). Although there is variation, because the authority in this system is vested in Washington, D.C., conditions in federal prisons are basically standardized. Depending on the security level, one facility is pretty much like another.

Historically, the FBOP was created to incarcerate gangsters, racketeers, kidnappers, bank robbers, drug smugglers, white collar criminals, tax protestors, and political subversives. Congress created the first federal prisons with the "Three Prisons Act" in 1891, which authorized the U.S. Department of Justice to establish three autonomous "big house" penitentiaries. For the next 30 years, most federal prisoners were held at Leavenworth (Kansas), Atlanta (Georgia), or McNeil Island (Washington).

In 1930, thanks to the *Mann Act of 1910* (against prostitution), the *Harrison Act of 1914* (narcotics), the *Volstead Act of 1919* (prohibition), the *Deyer Act of 1919* (interstate automobile theft), the beginning of the Great Depression, and the growth in organized crime, Congress passed legislation to create the FBOP. Prohibition provided Congress with the primary rationale for the first expansion of the federal prison system. The Bureau moved quickly by building another penitentiary at Lewisburg, Pennsylvania; hospital prisons at Springfield, Missouri; Lexington, Kentucky; and Ft. Worth, Texas; a youth reformatory at Chillicothe, Ohio; and a number of minimum security camps.

In 1984, at the start of the war on drugs, the entire system had only 32,000 prisoners. In 2001, the FBOP operated 96 prisons, with a total population exceeding 143,000. Approximately 20,000 of these men and women are "on the bus," in local jails, or confined in privately operated facilities. This growth is the result of more federal investigations, prosecutions, judicial activity, and new legislation that dramatically altered sentencing in the federal criminal justice system. Most of the Bureau's growth since the mid-1980s has been the result of the *Sentencing Reform Act of 1984*, which established determinate sentencing, abolished parole, and reduced good time (time off for good behavior), and the mandatory minimum sentences enacted in 1986, 1988, and 1990. The FBOP prisoner count is expected to grow to 200,000 over the next few years.

Federal Security Levels

The FBOP uses an "inmate classification system" as a means to segregate, control, punish, and reward prisoners. This is a ladder with maximum security at the top, and minimum security at the bottom. If the FBOP operated to facilitate rehabilitation (they don't), prisoners ideally would work their way down the ladder with good conduct and program participation. As they completed their sentences and got "short" (meaning a year to release), they would be moved to minimum security camps or community custody. But this is the real world, where more men and women move up the ladder from minimum to medium, or medium to maximum, rather than down. Few medium and maximum security prisoners ever make it to the minimum security camps.

Classification designations have changed over the years to serve the growth in FBOP prisons and population. The old system had six security levels, with 6–5 being maximum, 4–2 medium, and 1 being minimum security. USP Marion (the first supermax penitentiary) was the only level 6 institution. United States Penitentiaries were level 5 (e.g., USP Atlanta, USP Leavenworth, USP Lewisburg, USP Lom Poc); the Federal Correctional Institutions ranged from 4 to 2 (e.g., FCI Talledega, FCI Sandstone, FCI Oxford, etc.), and the Federal Prison Camps were 1.

In the 1990s, the FBOP collapsed these six security designations into five: high, medium high, medium low, minimum, and administrative. Today the FBOP prisoner population is approximately 10 percent high (USP), 25 percent high medium (FCI), 35 percent low medium (FCI), and 25 percent minimum (FPC), with the rest not assigned a security level; many of these men and women are in administrative facilities (medical or detention), transit, or held in local jails or private prisons (discussed later in this chapter). "Administrative" refers to Administrative Detention Max in ADX Florence, Colorado—the highest security prison in the country; FTC Oklahoma City (a medium security transport prison); and the federal medical centers, which may be maximum, medium, or minimum security.

The differences in security level reflect the crime and length of sentence. In general, maximum security is reserved for cons with long criminal histories, sentences, and histories of violence.

According to FBOP guidelines, you have to be 26 years old to go to a penitentiary; however, this doesn't mean that the FBOP always abides by their own guidelines. Medium security is for younger prisoners, doing more than 10 years. Minimum security is occupied by prisoners with sentences below 10 years and no indication of serious management problems.

Minimum Security

Federal Prison Camps (FPC) are minimum security facilities that are constructed of dormitories, some with fences, some without, that may be satellites to a neighboring FCI or USP, or stand alone. These camps, with populations ranging from a few hundred to several thousand, are the cheapest and least secure institutions. Many of the men or women who are serving their first prison sentence in these camps could easily be moved to probation or community facilities without any danger to the public. Minimum security camps and medium security correctional institutions are quite often the destination for many middle-class defendants (white collar, corporate, or drug offenses).

As prison sentences lengthen, many camps have been fenced in to stem the increasing problem with escapes, called "walk-aways." If a prisoner decides to leave camp in this manner or violate other minimum security regulations, he'll likely be promoted (kicked upstairs) to medium security.

Medium Security

Federal Correctional Institutions (FCI), populated by younger adult prisoners, are medium security prisons, with no walls, guarded by heavy razor wire fences and gun towers. Many of the newer institutions have modern pod architecture; separate buildings holding 200 prisoners in what the Bureau refers to as "unit management."

Medium security prisons, traditionally reformatories for young adult prisoners, have added security features like double fences, gun towers, and internal control architecture that resembles higher-security institutions. These "Gladiator schools," as the prisoners have dubbed them, can be very violent places. Young men tend to be the most volatile group of prisoners, engaging in constant fist fights, often as a way to work off their excess energy. Most guards, however, don't even know such fights take place, or by the time they find out about them, the fights are over. Fortunately, these altercations rarely result in a killing.

The Federal Bureau of Prisons distinguishes between low medium and high medium security prisons.

The old reformatories, built in the early 1900s, were meant to be junior penitentiaries with cellblocks of cages, industrial workshops, and some vocational and educational programs.

There are two styles of new construction for medium security institutions. The first one (e.g., Federal Correctional Institutions) is built of steel and concrete, with a yard and separate buildings for administrative offices, factories, recreation and programs, and housing convicts. The housing units are separate buildings, with individual pods, which house a few hundred prisoners each, and are usually one or two floors tall. These units organize prisoners into disciplinary steps, with each building representing different levels of privilege. For instance, there may be a building for Reception and Departure (R-and-D), a unit for new prisoners, and additional units for ascending levels of good behavior. In addition, each prison may have special cellblocks, called administrative segregation (AD SEG), or segregated housing units (SHU) for disciplinary violators (the hole), protective custody (PC), medical prisoners, gang isolation, or drug therapy. Prisoners are moved from one unit to another as they are evaluated, disciplined, or isolated as decided by the prison administration.

In contrast, many states are building a second style, which is basically a cheaper version of the first. These states are attempting to save on construction costs by building new medium security prisons of fabricated steel and concrete, with little stone or brick.

The buildings may resemble large farm sheds with few windows, actually large metal pole barns on a concrete foundation. These penal facilities are little more than human warehouses, consisting mostly of security perimeters and housing units. The institution may have no recreational yard or gym, factories, or programs. The prisoners live in vast dormitory-style housing units with hundreds of men sleeping on bunk beds, stacked two high, and arranged a few feet apart.

Regardless of the system, federal or state, the designation CI means that the facility is a medium security prison. Thus in Ohio an OCI, or Ohio Correctional Institution, is probably a medium security facility.

Medium security prisons hold populations of a few hundred to several thousand inmates. Housing units (the individual cellblocks or dormitories within the prison) may house 100 to 500 men in each.

Because of the chaotic confusion of living for years in huge open dormitories, these hastily constructed institutions are known in prison parlance as "bus stops," "pig pens," or "dog kennels." Many medium security prisoners are transferred to maximum security institutions for disciplinary infractions.

Maximum Security

Maximum security prisons can be divided into three categories: the old "Big House" penitentiaries, the new generation facilities, and the super-maximum institutions.

The Big Houses

The Big House penitentiaries, many of them built in the late nineteenth or early twentieth century, are fortress-like structures, enclosed by walls 30 to 50 feet high, with buildings made of stone, brick, concrete, and steel, containing massive cellblocks, some five tiers high. These ancient prisons are still operating, even as they are supplemented by the construction of modern penitentiaries.

USP Leavenworth, the oldest and most famous, and the "geographical center of the FBOP," is known for the advanced training in criminal occupations available from old cons; for example, bank robbery, securities fraud, or counterfeiting currency. This penitentiary can hold as many as 2,000 prisoners in four cell-houses (labeled A, B, C, and D) that each consists of five tiers stacked to a 150 foot ceiling. Protected by six gun towers, the prison walls are 35 feet high, 12 feet wide, and extend 35 feet into the ground to prevent tunneling. Leavenworth has no air-conditioning in the cell-blocks and is described as the "Hot House" because of the extreme temperatures endured by prisoners during the long Kansas summer. The cell-houses are also freezing cold in winter, with ice sometimes forming on the floor and walls.

These federal "pens" such as Leavenworth are reserved for older prisoners (at least 26 years of age, according to the guidelines) serving long sentences. A large number of the convicts in Leavenworth are older men, many of them having spent most of their lives incarcerated. Some are cold-blooded killers, some are violent psychopaths, while others just want to be left alone to do their time.

New Generation Pens

From a distance, the new generation penitentiaries may appear more like factories, but they are enclosed by heavy security fences and gun towers. There are no tall walls. The double or triple chain link perimeter fence is layered with rolls of razor wire that may carry an electric current and include remote sensors and video cameras to alert the guards of attempted escapes.

Inside, these correctional institutions may have a dining hall and "yard," and limited space designated for prisoner employment, recreation, or education. The housing units, like the many medium security prisons, are pod construction, which is expensive and requires separate structures, each with its own staff offices. Some of these pods may have separate rooms for one or two convicts, each with a metal door, half bath, and communal showers at the end of each tier.

Trustworthy prisoners may have keys to their rooms. In comparison, disciplinary prisoners may be locked in their rooms and fed meals through the door slot (wicket). Unit construction of concrete block walls and cement floors is generally considered by prisoners to be an improvement over traditional cellblocks of multiple iron cages.

Supermax and Administrative Detention

The FBOP takes pride in the Federal Correctional Complex at Florence, Colorado, which includes four new prisons: a minimum level camp, medium security correctional institution, maximum security penitentiary, and an administrative maximum detention facility. The Administrative Detention Maximum (ADX) at Florence is a supermax prison, colorfully labeled by the convicts, "the Hellhole of the Rockies." This is the highest-security prison in the system and replaced the supermax control unit at USP Marion (Illinois). Technically, the law provides that all prisoners in segregated housing units (SHU), control units (USP Marion), or supermax prisons (ADX Florence) must be released from their cells once a day for one hour of physical exercise. Nonetheless, there is no outside legal authority enforcing the rule. Therefore, in practice many prisoners spend 24 hours in their cells without their one hour of exercise. Even if they get the one hour, this, too, will be in solitary, and it allows the guards an opportunity to search the prisoners' cells.

Prison administrators (i.e., the Director of the FBOP and wardens) can transfer a convict from one institution to another without any official reason. For example, they can move an inmate to a medical facility without a doctor's recommendation, or to a supermax detention center without a disciplinary report. Prisoners sent to a supermax include those who have assaulted or killed other inmates or prison staff. Suspected gang leaders, political activists, or high-profile prisoners (e.g., the Unibomber, Timothy McVeigh, John Gotti, terrorists, and spies) also often end up in supermaxes. Prisoners do not have to be in violation of FBOP rules to be sent to a supermax. Once inside the supermax, their contact with others is severely limited. They are allowed few outside visitors and have limited phone and mail privileges.

ADX Florence, like the USP Marion control unit, and the administrative segregation units (the hole) in the "mainline" penitentiaries (e.g., USP Leavenworth, USP Atlanta, USP Lewisburg), enforces a strict discipline with few privileges.

You enter ADX Florence by descending a 50-foot staircase. The prison cellblocks are located below ground level. The facility has 550 permanently locked-down one-man cells, but only half the cells are occupied. The empty cells are reserved for intake prisoners who may be transferred in from rebellious or rioting institutions. Prisoners eat all their meals in their concrete "boxcar" cells, leaving only to exercise in a private room an hour per day (if they're lucky). The prison staff can use four-point spread-eagle restraints, forced feedings, cell extractions (forceful removal), mind control medications, and nonlethal chemical weapons to incapacitate resistant prisoners.

ADX Florence was built not only to eliminate escapes, but also to defend from outside attack. At all medium and maximum security facilities, the "outrider" (a guard who patrols outside the fence or wall) is usually a correctional officer in a pick-up truck armed with a shotgun, who drives around the prison perimeter. The ADX Florence outrider vehicle is an armored personnel carrier (similar to a tank without a cannon) occupied by three guards carrying automatic weapons whose duties include demanding identification from visitors.

Many states are building supermax institutions modeled after the USP Marion and ADX Florence.

Other Prison Facilities

Medium and maximum security prisons may have special cell-blocks, units, or dormitories for prisoners with chronic or acute problems; for example, the elderly, medical or mentally disabled, or sexually deviant. Some correctional systems have separate hospital prisons for elderly or medical convictions (e.g., Federal Medical Centers). Many prisons have entire cellblocks occupied by prisoners who have HIV or AIDS, are mentally retarded or mentally ill, or are homosexual.

Federal Medical Centers are either camps (FMC Rochester), correctional institutions (FMC Lexington), or penitentiaries (MCFP Springfield) housing convicts at different security levels, and are staffed by U.S. Public Health medical staff. These institutions are used for elderly, ill, and dying prisoners. Each of these medical prisons houses hundreds of men in wheelchairs, dying from cancer, AIDS, or other serious illnesses.

When a prisoner dies, from old age or infirmities, he is placed on a stretcher with wrists handcuffed and leg irons on his ankles, wheeled down the corridor, and transported to a nearby private hospital and declared dead on arrival. This administrative gimmick allows the FBOP to seriously underreport the number of prisoners who expire in their custody. (Not that any such tricks are really needed, since the constituency for old cons who die in prison is virtually nil.) There is no funeral. The body is photographed with handcuffs and leg irons still on. If the prisoner has not made alternate arrangements, he is usually buried in the prison graveyard.

Metropolitan Correctional Centers (MCC) are high-rise prisons that resemble corporate office buildings, with many of them located in large cities (e.g., MCC New York, MCC Chicago). The roofs are used for helicopter pads and exercise areas for prisoners. These facilities serve as both prison and courthouse. Many federal prisoners are housed at an MCC during trials, either as witnesses or when being charged with new indictments.

In addition, the Bureau operates Federal Detention Centers (FDC) and Metropolitan Detention Centers (MDC), which are prisons for foreign citizens who have completed their FBOP sentences and are being deported to their home countries. In 1986, just months after it was opened, FDC Oakdale (Louisiana) was burned to the ground by Cuban prisoners.

Probably the most unique prison in the FBOP is the Federal Transport Center (FTC) at Oklahoma City. This facility processes thousands of convicts each year who arrive and depart on Federal Marshal prison planes and buses. It has a runway that allows jet airliners transporting prisoners to taxi up to the security fence, where convicts deplane to be taken inside the correctional institution.

Private Versus Public Prisons

Many states and the federal government have experimented with private jails and prisons operated by for-profit corporations. Regardless of the fact that they are owned and operated by corporations, they are all funded with taxpayer money.

Private prisons, like chain gangs and boot camps, are nothing new. They have been tried before. After the Civil War, a number of southern states sentenced prisoners to plantation-type prisons operated by private companies. This was part of what became known as the "convict-leasing system" whereby prisoners, many of them former slaves, were locked up in prison camps and contracted out as rent-a-slaves back to the cotton, rice, and sugar cane plantations. Private companies, contractors, and rich landowners made a bundle under this arrangement, while the prisoners suffered. This practice continues in many southern states. Remember the Paul Newman film *Cool Hand Luke?*

The recent growth in private prisons has not improved the conditions of confinement. These facilities, although they may be new, and even attempt correctional innovations, only house a small percentage of the national prison population. Typically, a private company operates one or two experimental facilities in a given state for only minimum security prisoners. To date, there are no private maximum security facilities in the United States. This whole process is called "creaming the population," where a corporation builds a facility and contracts to take assignment of only short-term nonviolent convicts.

Even so, despite having the luxury of only having to deal with "lightweight" prisoners, private prisons have had their share of problems, including escapes, violence, riots, and rising expenses. Typically, corporations designed these facilities to be "cost effective," profitable for shareholders by paying lower wages to less qualified and poorly trained nonunion staff, bare bones programming, and meager spending on educational, vocational, recreational, and medical services.

Numerous studies carried out by the U.S. General Accounting Office, U.S. Marshals Service, Immigration and Naturalization Service, and the Urban Institute have reported that it actually costs the taxpayer more to incarcerate individuals in private rather than public facilities. In fact, the cost can be at least 10 percent more per prisoner per day, and considerably more in the long run, once additional public expenses are factored in.

In the final analysis, private prisons reduce public accountability, increase government liability, and drive up the cost of incarceration. Meanwhile, private ownership and operation of correctional facilities raise difficult Constitutional issues and legal concerns that have yet to be resolved and have promulgated a plethora of lawsuits. Finally, in a democratic society, do we really want private corporations to profit from imprisonment?

Going "Up the River"

It's only logical that Prison World USA should have its own transportation net, one that reaches from coast to coast and border to border.

Most federal prisoners are transported from county jails or state or military prisons "up the river" (an expression dating back to when prisoners went up the Hudson River to New York State's Sing Sing prison) into the federal system by U.S. Marshals in cars, buses, or planes. A few are allowed to "self-surrender" at camps. Prisoners refer to prison transports as "con-air," "dog buses," "diesel therapy," or "bus therapy." Prisoners are subject to numerous transports, most of them unwelcome, as they are transferred from one institution to another across the country.

The FBOP transports 40 prisoners on Greyhound-type buses that have blacked out windows secured with iron bars. These vehicles cruise the nation's interstate highway system, stopping along their routes at lockups to pick up or drop off prisoners. They only travel during the day, and might be escorted by security or chase cars. On board, the prisoners wear khaki uniforms, paper slippers instead of shoes, leg irons, and handcuffs attached to belly chains. High-security prisoners wear double handcuffs and "black boxes," a device worn over the handcuffs to prevent picking locks. State prisoners are transported less often, and for fewer miles.

Prison transports are always tense. FBOP buses are staffed with three guards: a driver, and two more officers who occupy gun cages at the front and back of the vehicle. The officers are usually armed with pistol-grip short-barrel pump shotguns. They are responsible for the loading, transport, and delivery of prisoners. They do not tolerate interference with their duties during the long trips. There are no stops for food or restrooms. Prisoners are expected to use the bus toilet while still in restraints. (It's not unusual to see men wet their pants.) The bus trips are especially dangerous for elderly or medically frail prisoners. Statistics on the number of men and women who have died on these transports are unavailable from the FBOP.

In addition to buses, the FBOP, like in the movie *Con Air*, has its own fleet of airliners. These large jets have been converted, much as the buses, to fit the requirements of prisoner transport.

The FBOP operates its own mini-airports all over the country where prisoners are transferred from buses to be airlifted to the next destination. These planes are used to transport as many as 90 prisoners at a time from one part of the country to another. Generally, prisoners prefer airlift to buses, as the duress and duration of the trip is less.

The FBOP has even invented a new kind of prison—federal transport centers (FTCs) devoted exclusively to transporting prisoners. For example, FTC Oklahoma City is a medium security prison where FBOP planes land and taxi through areas surrounded by razor wire fence to unload their prisoners inside a giant hangar within the prison.

According to the FBOP, prisoners may request transfers to be "closer to home," to receive medical attention at a federal medical center (e.g., MCFP Springfield, FMC Rochester, FMC Fort Worth, FMC Lexington), or for participation in institutional programs (e.g., education, prison industries). The FBOP also uses frequent transfers to discipline prisoners, redistribute population to new or less crowded facilities, racially balance institutions, and protect snitches. Another common reason is to disable or obstruct convict legal talent. Prisoners who file Administrative Remedy paperwork (called BPs), to report their complaints or concerns, or as a prerequisite for filing lawsuits or motions to court, are routinely treated to a trip on the "writ bus."

These jailhouse lawyers may ride the bus back and forth across the country, along the way staying in different prisons for many months. The FBOP transfers inmate litigants out of their federal court district as a means to kill their legal motions. Some of the prisoners are disbarred attorneys, while most are convicts who have educated themselves in legal procedures. FBOP functionaries will do what it takes to discourage these men from filing legal briefs, including locking them up in segregated housing units (SHU) or administrative super-maximum prisons (ADX Florence).

Transfers

The FBOP transports thousands of prisoners every week. Every night these men and women, who are officially called "holdover" prisoners, are housed in different prisons. Various federal prisons provide different accommodations for these "guests." If there is room available in the penitentiaries and correctional institutions, they are usually confined in "holdover units," "bus stops" (dormitories for new prisoners), R-and-D (receiving and departure) holding cells, or administrative detention (the hole). If the prison is already crowded (no empty beds), they will either sleep on the bus or on mattresses laid out in corridors on cell-house tiers. In camps, the visiting prisoners may sleep in crowded dorms, hallways, or recreational areas.

Transport and holdover prisoners travel with the clothes they wear and their one "federal box," which holds all of their belongings and is loaded in the cargo bay of the bus or plane. While in transit, which may last for weeks or months, prisoners normally do not receive mail, have access to phones, or opportunities for outside visits. They do not work, participate in prison programs, receive institutional pay, or have commissary privileges. They are denied regular communication with the outside world (family, friends, press, and legal representatives). They are forced to depend on the generosity of general population prisoners for necessary items— soap, shampoo, smokes—which may or may not be forthcoming.

In contrast to federal prisoners, who may be transported across the United States, state prisoners are usually subject to shorter trips. Generally, state prisoners are taken in police cars, school buses converted for prison use, or vans. These trips are usually from county jail to prison. Because state systems are smaller, these prisoners may serve time in fewer prisons; thus they are transferred less frequently.

Propaganda Versus Reality

The FBOP prides itself on operating orderly institutions, but Bureau propaganda doesn't always match the reality. Many of the older federal prisons are plagued by overcrowding, understaffing, convict violence, and rampant staff corruption including theft of food, building supplies, and tools. A dinner menu change or mess hall food shortage may be the result of thieving guards or incompetent administrators. Like the cons, the guards, too, operate in cliques, with many of them blood relatives or related by marriage, and, like the cons, they sometimes cover for each other. Despite the best efforts of internal affairs officers, cons and guards (often acting in concert) continue their illegal activities.

Chapter 4

Hacks, Cops, and Cons: Who's Who in Prison

Prisons are commonly referred to as "total institutions," which are not only paramilitary in terms of the chain of command, but are bureaucratic like big government institutions. A total institution is one in which almost every aspect of an individual's life is provided for and controlled by the organization. This is similar to a monastery, mental hospital, or army, all three of which share many features in common with prison.

Within the prison there are two mutually antagonistic groups, the convicts, who have almost no contact with the outside world, and the staff who supervise them, who get to go home to the real world at the end of each workday. Each interprets the other in terms of stereotypes. Cons see guards as authoritarian and stupid, the hated soldiers guarding prisoners of a foreign army. Guards see cons as untrustworthy, vicious, criminal scum.

Who's Doing Time?

The federal prisoner population is 92 percent male, 50 percent white, the rest being black, Hispanic, Asian, Native American, or "other." The FBOP reports that 70 percent of prisoners are American citizens, with 20 percent being Mexican, Colombian, or Cuban, and 10 percent unknown or from other countries. Seventy-five percent of these men and women are serving sentences of over five years, with nearly 50 percent doing 10 years or more. Fifty-eight percent are doing time for drug convictions. The average age of a federal prisoner is 37 years old.

All federal convicts have a "jacket," which refers to their official prison file, which includes their pre-sentence investigation (PSI Report), commitment papers, and institutional records. Each prison keeps large loose-leaf notebooks containing mug shot photos of each prisoner.

The FBOP Central Inmate Monitoring System (CIMS) is a computer program that tracks nine special categories of prisoners:

- **Witness Security** prisoners are government informers who did, are, or will testify in court cases.

- **Special Security** refers to prison snitches cooperating in internal investigations.

- **Sophisticated Criminal Activity** identifies cons involved in large-scale criminal conspiracies, for example organized crime, drugs, or white collar. They may be men or women who were targets of federal "Racketeer Influence and Corrupt Organization" (RICO) or "Continuing Criminal Enterprise" (CCE) prosecution, which carry life sentences. Many of these convicts are thought to be persons connected to major drug-smuggling organizations, who refused to plead guilty, cooperate, or inform on other persons.

- **Threats to Government Officials** covers prisoners convicted of writing letters, making phone calls, or issuing verbal remarks that convey the intent to do bodily harm to public officials.

- **Broad Publicity** prisoners are those who are featured in high-profile cases that have received a lot of media attention.

This may include, for example, a former U.S. Attorney convicted of selling heroin, or the Attorney General of a state serving time for bribery.

■ **State Prisoners** are difficult convicts serving state sentences who were transferred into the federal system. Gang leaders, prisoners convicted of violent offences against staff or other convicts, or those with histories of prison escapes are transferred into the FBOP. This may include juvenile prisoners from state prisons, covered in tattoos, who because of their institutional history of violence had been reassigned to the FBOP.

■ **Separation** requires that persons who are government witnesses, institutional snitches, gang leaders, or are in danger of being killed or killing someone else be moved to another incarceration.

■ **Special Supervision** prisoners are cops, judges, and politicians and are provided protective privilege. These men and women are usually assigned to camps; they would not survive long in a penitentiary.

■ **Disruptive Groups** may include members of organizations, such as street or prison gangs and political subversives.

An Alternative Classification

The official FBOP classification of prisoners is designed to separate prisoners into security levels. In comparison, we suggest that an alternative system may prove useful when thinking about different groups of prisoners: amateur, professional, reservation, and political.

Amateurs are persons with only a part-time or occasional involvement with criminal activities. These are men and women, many of them married with families, who held legitimate employment and lived conventional lives before imprisonment. Most federal prisoners convicted of petty property crimes or minor drug offenses are amateurs. Some of them are serving short sentences for minor offenses, such as failure to pay student loans or income tax, Social Security fraud, or violation of immigration laws. This is the largest group of prisoners. The longer they stay in prison, however, the more likely they are to learn and assume the ways and means of professional crime.

Professionals are prisoners who, when they lived in the "free world," had occupational positions that required special training and experience, be it legal or illegal. For example, doctors, lawyers, politicians, and corporate personnel, as well as successful drug smugglers, bank robbers, organized criminals, or counterfeiters are professionals. In prison you may find cops, judges, and attorneys, as well as ministers, priests, doctors, dentists, bankers, stockbrokers, elected officials, even university professors. One measure of professionalism, whether illicit or legitimate, is the income or fortune derived from employment. FBOP prisons contain numerous individuals who were considered "pros" because of the resources and assets they retained from either legal or illegal enterprises.

Reservation refers to land reserved for federal uses. All crimes committed on Indian reservations or military property, or within the District of Columbia (D.C.) come under federal jurisdiction. Native American, military, and D.C. residents, convicted of crimes on federal property, are considered reservation prisoners. The FBOP is home to many Native Americans, military personnel, and D.C. residents, who find themselves incarcerated in distant federal prisons for relatively minor offenses, such as misdemeanors. They usually are serving relatively short sentences compared to the typical federal convict. For example, Native Americans sentenced for drunk driving or petty theft usually spend less than a year in prison and are then released back to the reservation.

The FBOP is also receiving an increasing number of military prisoners, many of them transferred in from the Leavenworth Detention Barracks (KS), Army Stockades, or Navy Brigs. A common complaint of such prisoners is that FBOP inmate law libraries do not have the military case law reference material needed for them to fight their criminal cases or pursue appellate remedies.

The D.C. prisoners, coming primarily from the more disadvantaged neighborhoods of Washington, D.C., are an ongoing headache for the FBOP. Both guards and convicts use "DCers," in a derogatory fashion, to indicate that they are serving relatively short sentences for common street crimes. These prisoners are shipped in from "the District," Maryland, and Virginia jails and prisons. They are held under unique legal provisions that provide for parole, assuming they do not catch additional time or lose "good time," while imprisoned in the FBOP.

The FBOP also imprisons a number of political types who have violated federal laws in the furtherance of their various causes. Coming from all parts of the political spectrum, they include abortion clinic bombers, anti-nuclear activists, environmentalists, subversives, socialists, communists, anarchists, militia members, neo-Nazis, extremist and hate groups, etc. Activists who write press releases, have constituencies, and hold some measure of public credibility are viewed with a jaundiced eye by the FBOP.

The Color Line

The primary dividing line in prison populations is racial. With few exceptions, black prisoners associate with blacks, whites with whites, and Hispanics with Hispanics. In some facilities, especially those with violent criminals, hostilities between the three groups may be such that a convict who strays into the turf of a group not his own may suffer beatings, rape, even death. Some prison administrators may use racial conflict as a means to divide and conquer the inmate population.

Alternatively, in some overcrowded, understaffed institutions, the authorities sometimes make a kind of Faustian bargain, allowing one or more violent cliques to dominate the rest of the prison population and maintain internal order and discipline.

Special, fascinating variant subgenres include those from the subterranean worlds of organized crime, big-time drug smugglers moving major weight (thousands of kilos of drugs), and motorcycle gangs.

✗ Prisoners of the Drug Wars

International drug smugglers comprise a unique and powerful prison subculture. As long as there have been governments in existence to prohibit certain goods, there have been those willing to take risks to supply the contraband. In the past, contraband has included such diverse substances and goods as salt, Venetian glass, silks, laces, brandy, Port wines, coffee, tea, and more recently in the failed American experiment known as Prohibition, alcoholic beverages.

Kings of contraband today are illegal drugs, such as marijuana, cocaine, heroin, ecstasy, and methamphetamines. Illegal drugs generate tremendous profits. These federal prisoners of the drug war include smugglers, pilots, and boat crew members.

While they have been convicted of crimes, many of them do not consider themselves criminals per se, any more than Elizabethan Era Sea Hawk privateers such as Drake, Hawkins, or Frobisher were considered pirates for preying on Spanish galleons. Their modern-day counterparts are a restless breed, many of them adrenaline addicts with a liking for foreign travel and adventure and a need for high-risk, profit-making ventures. Some were Vietnam veterans, even war heroes, others mercenaries or soldiers of fortune. Some were well educated, multilingual, and rich. They did not and do not consider themselves "criminals," and in prison, Napoleon's dictum holds true: "In war, the moral is to the material as three to one."

North American Anglo (English-speaking) smugglers worked closely with their Caribbean, Mexican, Central and South American partners. Hispanic-Latino drug soldiers saw nothing wrong in supplying gringos' voracious appetites for drugs. The Colombian cartel employees, many of them middle or upper class, educated in America or Europe, consider themselves to be "trade representatives." Apart from being a vehicle to amass fabulous personal riches in a relatively short time span (if one is not convicted or, more likely, killed), the Colombians considered it their patriotic duty to market their national agricultural products and return to their country with investment capital so they could sponsor economic development.

The Colombians tend to be more serious, successful, and businesslike than their Cuban, Jamaican, and Mexican counterparts, who may have also been their colleagues or competitors in smuggling operations. A keystone of their success is their well-deserved reputation for ultra-violence in pursuit of their profitable trade. When they kill, they often take out not only the object of their disaffection, but any family members, servants, or anybody else unlucky enough to be on the premises when the strike is made.

Violence is endemic throughout the drug trade, to eliminate competition and discourage informers and hijackers. The more spectacular and memorable the violence, the more successful it is in spreading terror, which cuts down on future problems.

The National Crime Syndicate

A second subgroup, which for decades has been an important element of federal prison populations, are the members of organized crime, the national crime syndicate which includes the Mafia. Among them are the soldiers, managers, executives, and directors of an extensive criminal empire controlling vast sections of the American and indeed, the global, economy. They are the big and not-so-big gangsters who run the rackets in America.

Bikers

A third group consists of the bikers, members of the Hell's Angels, Outlaws, Diablos, Satan's Slaves, Pagans, and other assorted motorcycle clubs. Outlaw motorcycle clubs can be thought of as the light cavalry of organized crime. Such gangs figure prominently in the drug trade, specializing in the making and distribution of amphetamines and other "speed"-type drugs, and in prostitution rings associated with females employed at strip joints.

The U.S. Department of Justice specializes in prosecuting bikers, according to bikers, and the FBOP confines thousands of these men and their female associates in its penal institutions. They were, and in many cases still are, the most significant gang population in many federal penitentiaries (for more on gangs, see Chapter 9, "Blood In, Blood Out: Prison Gangs and Violence").

The Aryan Brotherhood (AB) or Nation is viewed as the most dangerous convict organization in federal prison. First formed in 1968 from the ranks of Hell's Angels and Blue Bird gang members in San Quentin, and spreading rapidly through the prisons of the West and Southwest, they were designed as a counterforce to the numerically superior black and Hispanic gangs' domination over minority white prison populations.

According to prison legend, there is only one way in or out of this gang: blood in, blood out. Convicts become AB members by committing murder, and only leave the organization upon their own death. They are known for being tattooed with swastikas, SS lightning bolts, and the so-called Number of the Beast, 666. Today, many members of the AB are locked up in supermax federal prisons (e.g., ADX Florence or the control units in USP Marion).

Each of the subgroups provide a unique support system in prison, but it's a members-only support system. You are not one of them, or else you would not be reading and needing this book. Maintaining cordial, correct, and respectfully distant relations with such groups is recommended, where feasible. For outsiders, involvement in their schemes and intrigues may prove to be a potential minefield.

The Living Dead

In the United States, people convicted of committing capital or other extremely serious crimes can be sentenced to death. The federal government and most states (38) have the death penalty. The only jurisdictions (13 in total) that don't have the death penalty are Alaska, District of Columbia, Hawaii, Iowa, Maine, Massachusetts, Michigan, Minnesota, North Dakota, Rhode Island, Vermont, West Virginia, and Wisconsin. Some states that have the death penalty on the books don't have any convicts on "death row" (so named because of the long hallway the person is usually kept in). For example, in 1996, Kansas, New Hampshire, New York, and Wyoming lacked death row convicts. California, Texas, and Florida have the highest number of death row inmates.

Since 1930, state and federal governments have executed over 4,300 people, and since 1977 Texas has lead the way in those executions, with approximately 144. Prisoners given the death penalty typically have to wait a little over seven years before their sentence is carried out. In the meantime, they and their lawyers usually appeal their sentence on a number of grounds. Despite the numerous stays of execution, most death row inmates eventually are killed. In some states, the governor can intervene and commute death sentences to life without parole.

Most death row convicts are male and black. About half of all death row inmates never married, and about 25 percent are widowed, divorced, or separated (which says a lot about their own or their loved ones' confidence that they'll one day actually get out of prison). Less than half of the prisoners facing death have a high school education, and over half of them are between the ages of 20 and 39. Few death row convicts are women—approximately 44 women wait on death row today.

Death row prisoners can "meet their maker" in one of five ways. The most prominent means of execution is by lethal injection, with 27 states killing prisoners this way. Other methods include electrocution (12 states), gas chambers (7), hanging (4), and firing squads (3). Prisoners are usually given a choice between lethal injection or one of the other execution techniques. Since 1977 most people (406) have been killed by lethal injection.

Contrary to popular belief, most research indicates that the death penalty doesn't serve as a crime deterrent. People also consider the death penalty to be a form of payback, or "just deserts," for the heinous crimes the prisoner might have committed. Others think that killing an individual for a crime they committed, no matter how terrible it was, is barbaric and has no place in an advanced democracy. Many of those same people are happy to dismiss this drawback (and others) of the death penalty, when it comes to serial killers (e.g., Ted Bundy), mass murderers (Pol Pot), or terrorists (Osama bin Laden).

Prison Administration

When you first enter prison, you will be processed, "dressed out," and escorted to your housing units by officers. Although they'll wear uniforms and act like soldiers, it won't be clear to you what their rank is, or more importantly, who is really in charge. The big boss in any prison system is the State Director of the Department of Corrections who keeps a large staff in the state capital. Wardens, however, run the prisons, with the line of command being associate warden, assistant warden, major, captain, lieutenant, sergeant, and line officer. All prisons have two lines of command structure: the uniformed employees who guard prisoners and function as cops, and the case managers, counselors, program staff, and prison industries.

Hacks and Cops

Most of the time you will be ordered around by mere officers, only seeing the brass when you are in trouble, including heading for the "hole." Typically, the higher the rank, the less they want to talk with convicts. A cell-house or housing unit may have a sergeant and line officers on duty, changing on eight-hour shifts.

One of the first lessons you learn in prison is that you cannot judge people by the uniform they wear. Some convicts are honorable and decent persons, while others are not. The same can be said of the guards, a number of whom come to work every day and treat prisoners with courtesy and respect. One of the first things you have to do is figure out which officers to avoid.

Correctional officers are known as "hacks" or "cops" by the prisoners. A "hack" is an officer who collects his or her paycheck, does as little as possible, and goes home. A "cop" is a guard who is always on patrol trying to bust prisoners for petty infractions of the rules. According to the cons, most guards are hacks, some are cops, and a few are relatively decent types who actually try to relate to and help prisoners. A cop will send you to the hole and another officer, a man who deserves your thanks, will get you out. The best officers are men and women who keep their cool and behave humanely. Some few correctional officers have been known to risk their careers and the wrath of jail or prison administrators to defend the best interests of prisoners.

Power of Correctional Officers

At correctional facilities, cons outnumber guards. In most prisons, correctional officers are prohibited from carrying firearms or batons inside the prison. So why are the guards able to run the cons, rather than vice versa? As a group, guard training, organization, and discipline helps them control the convicts.

When it comes to maintaining order behind bars, guards have considerable powers, and can enforce their will without necessarily having to resort to force or violence. They attempt to run the prison on a system of rewards and punishments. Every facility has a long list of rules and regulations, and guards can enforce or ignore violations they see take place. Some of the benefits that they can offer, besides not strictly enforcing the rules, are choice job assignments, favorable reports, and responding to reasonable requests.

As previously noted, in overcrowded or understaffed prisons, the administration may give favorable treatment to a ruling clique or gang of prisoners in return for their keeping the other cons in the cellblocks in line. The racial divisions that may be found in prison populations may also help the administration keep the convicts under control, via the classic divide-and-rule strategy. Snitches, too, are an important tool used by the authorities to keep abreast of what's cooking among the cons.

Guards have been known to be co-opted, compromised, corrupted, or directly involved in illegal acts, like smuggling contraband into prison, covering up violent incidents, or looking the other way when prisoners are breaking serious official rules. Society is notoriously stingy when it comes to paying those charged with overseeing imprisoned lawbreakers, and low-paid guards may be susceptible to the lure of easy money.

Many correctional officers suffer from being alienated, cynical, burned out, or stressed out. Just like convicts, guards have their own cliques and gangs. In many states and the federal system, they learn to do their job through a training academy and through observing senior officers on the job. Senior guards teach them how to "read" convicts, sniff out trouble, and control cellblocks. Contrary to convict gospel, guards don't necessarily hate inmates, although first-hand exposure to some of the more vicious prisoners under their control tends to promote cynicism and contempt.

Mainly, being a correctional officer is a job, and the guards just want to get through their daily shifts with no hassles. They don't like problems and they'll come down hard on prisoners who they perceive as problem-causing troublemakers.

Are guards employed in an occupation or a profession? Are they white-collar or blue-collar workers? The cons would describe them as militarized factory workers. Guards are poorly paid and need to meet only basic educational requirements. Few people would consider working in prisons a high-status job. Surveys of the American public consistently show that low numbers have considered working as correctional officers. This is usually attributed to the fact that working as a guard is perceived to be one of the less glamorous aspects of law enforcement. Of course, other polls would show that few members of the public have considered working as garbage collectors, but society can't function without them, either. The difference is that garbage collectors are generally better paid and enjoy better working conditions than prison guards.

Still, most guards are persons with few career alternatives. Correctional workers have low occupational opportunities, usually do not like the employment, want as much as possible to get out and find another job, or dream about retirement. Often they work long hours for low pay.

In many institutions the guards complain that the bureaucratic rules are too numerous and changing all the time, which makes their job with the prisoners more difficult. Most correctional facilities have high rates of guard absenteeism, "sick days," and high turnover of personnel. And the only time the public spares them a thought is when there's a prison escape or riot. The best way that guards can make a respectable income is through putting in large amounts of overtime, a goal that is fast being brought into reach, thanks to America's ever-growing prison populations.

Case Managers and Counselors

Prison case managers may be men or women. They have college degrees, wear suits, have offices, and handle inmate paperwork. They keep the inmate files and process prisoners in and out of the institution. They are middle-management employees training to be wardens. They have a lot of power over you, as they control your housing assignment, the type of work you can do, visiting list, and access to programs like education, vocational training, and furloughs. They can help or hurt you, so it is important to keep your cool in their office and not invite their displeasure. Some of these prison executives work hard, and may do a good job of expediting your requests. Others are overwhelmed by their duties and may not respond at all, or in a delayed fashion. This can be particularly frustrating when you need them to execute your release documents.

Counselors usually handle personal property, legal mail, convict complaints, and disciplinary hearings. In most prisons a counselor is an older guard with limited formal education who wears a uniform, is usually a sergeant, and who sits in an office and runs interference for the case managers. The counselor is not your friend, or even a therapist. Make no mistake: Despite their job titles, counselors do not advise, counsel, or hold your hand.

Program staff may also include prison employees and contract workers who provide vocational, educational, or medical services. They may wear guard uniforms or civilian dress. Some consider themselves as part of the prison command structure, others as outsiders in some conflict with administrative norms. As correctional programs are very limited and have low administrative priority, don't expect much from program staff, as this can lead to frustration. After all, most prison programs are mere window dressing, designed as busy work, to maintain the prison or comply with legal mandates.

Most large prisons now have prison industries staffed by a combination of guards and corporate managers. The officers who work in these factories may wear a different uniform. For example, in the FBOP the federal prison industries (UNICOR) officers dress in gray work clothes, and look and may act like factory foremen. Still, they are officers, and when required, respond to security threats or disturbances like "line" hacks.

One new innovation in prison is the employment of women in mens' prisons. Today, females are working even in high-security correctional institutions, not only as program staff and administrators, but guarding men, too. These "lady hacks" may be well liked, even popular with the male convicts. At the very least, their presence breaks up the monotony of the day for the men.

Hacks and cons both serve time in prison. Although the guards go home after their shift, they, too, suffer from prison hostilities: overcrowding of prisoners and poor working conditions.

Part 3

Doing Time

Chapter 5

Jugged: Welcome to Prison

Hell is other people, as Sartre observed—an insight you will soon appreciate on a visceral level, should you be so unfortunate as to wind up doing time in prison. Having seen how rough the law can play, will it surprise you to learn that the prison population also plays a mean game of hardball?

Your experience in prison will depend on who you are (age, education, physical size, gender, sexual orientation, criminal history), your crime, sentence, and the security level of the facility. But everyone goes through the same routine upon arrival in prison, and everyone must acquaint themselves with two sets of rules if they want to survive: the convict's code and the prison's rules.

Receiving and Departure

Upon arrival at the prison, you and your fellow fish, as new prisoners are called, are marched inside and go through R-and-D (not research and development, but Receiving and Departure), where you will be strip-searched, deloused, and issued a uniform. Then you are placed in a holding cell, called a "bullpen" or a "fish tank," reserved for new prisoners.

You'll be issued what's called a "set up," including bedding (two sheets, a pillowcase, and a blanket), toiletries (consisting of a bar of soap, toothpaste, and toothbrush), and a uniform consisting of cheaply made shoes, underwear, and a jumpsuit.

Well into the first half of the twentieth century, convicts wore striped clothing. This helped to identify prisoners if they tried to escape. The types of stripes (vertical or horizontal) and the combinations (e.g., vertical on pants and horizontal on shirts) also denoted the privileges and seniority of convicts. Later, prison "blues" and jumpsuits or overalls were introduced. Prison blues are usually cheap work clothes made of cotton denim. Jumpsuits come in a variety of different colors (orange, red, and white) and usually denote the pod or unit in the facility in which a prisoner is housed. This alternative to bar coding is useful for correctional officers in determining if a convict is not where he is supposed to be in the facility, and/or if he has to be escorted back to his appropriate cellhouse. Federal convicts are dressed out in worn military fatigues, some of which is army surplus.

You might also be issued a plastic ID card with your inmate number and photograph. It will resemble those issued to university staff and students, corporate employees, or government workers. The cards are used as identification at commissary and sick call, and to verify controlled movement throughout the penitentiary. Depending upon the relative sophistication of the technology employed, some prisons even require prisoners to wear these cards fastened to their uniforms, where they are displayed for staff or surveillance cameras to read. The cards may also be used in vending or copy machines, telephones, and housing units to open doors.

Once dressed out, you'll be fingerprinted, have your mug shot taken, and ordered to undress for a strip search. You will be told to stand with your back against a wall and face a correctional officer. The guard will order you to open your mouth and show your teeth, run your hands through your hair, show the backside of each ear, lift your penis and testicles, then turn around and face the wall, lift your feet, and bend over and spread the cheeks of your buttocks. Each time a prisoner is transferred in or out of a new prison, he goes through this routine.

Orientation and Fish Tier

In some joints, there may be a rudimentary orientation program, where you, one of the new fish, are issued an inmate rule book and allowed to ask questions. These sessions are essentially dog and pony shows; most new inmates learn the rules and procedures from other convicts.

As a new prisoner, you are technically unclassified, have not yet received a work assignment, and are not allowed phone or commissary privileges. You are typically locked down 24 hours a day on the fish tier. You may be under the misguided impression that the institution has a legal obligation to let you out of your cell for at least an hour. Being unclassified means that you are not a general population prisoner, which means you have few privileges and are subject to the same administrative procedures as convicts in segregated housing units. So do not expect to get outdoor exercise on the yard.

In some prisons, you might be kept locked in your cell for the first few days, until you acclimate to your new surroundings. Meanwhile, the guards check their computers and decide which dormitory or cellblock is appropriate or available for your assignment. Where you end up depends upon your age, race, sentence, and crime. For example, if you have been convicted of a violent crime or received a long sentence, you may go directly to the hole. On the other hand, if you are under 18, have declared yourself gay, or appear particularly vulnerable, you may be locked up in Protective Custody (PC).

Your new housing quarters may be a maximum security cellblock, five tiers high, holding 500 men; a medium security unit or pod with 100 or more rooms, each with two or more men; or a minimum security dormitory.

You'll be introduced to your new cellmates, who will probably begin sizing you up, trying to figure out whether you are friend or foe. After surviving your first terrifying 24 hours at the institution, you will gradually meet a cast of characters that includes fellow convicts, correctional officers, and administrators—citizens of a new world which operates by a different set of rules. Although most of these are written in a prisoner handbook, discussed in prisoner orientation sessions, related by fellow convicts, and/or posted on a bulletin board, only a slow process of trial and error will reveal the true nature of what privileges and duties are relegated to the individual convict.

If one is available, you will also be given a job. You will be assigned to the worst work detail; for example, 12 hours a day washing dishes or cleaning bathrooms. It may take as much as a month or more before your case manager gets around to your initial interview, which will be your first opportunity to request another job. This will also be your first chance to ask that your commissary and phone accounts be opened (more on commissary in Chapter 7, "My Baloney Has a First Name: Food in Prison").

Prison Friendships

During the first few weeks, you will stick out as a new prisoner. Some men will offer help or tell you what to do. Listen closely, as most of this unsolicited advice is well intended and will keep you out of a jam with convicts and staff. Generally, other convicts will prompt you to talk or shut up, tell you what to do when approached by other prisoners or officers, and show you where to line up to stand for counts, get fresh clothes and linens, or eat. In time, you may recognize that one or a small group of convicts are looking after you, providing correct information, and preventing you from stumbling into obvious trouble.

More than likely, these new friends will bunk nearby in your cell-house or dormitory. At first you may think you don't have very much in common with them, but this will change over time. Close proximity in living quarters is more important than age, race, or social class. These men will become your buddies—the fellows with whom you run day to day, keep company, and share information. If you are lucky, are well connected, or have exceptional social skills, your friends will back you up in disputes, take your side, and provide some measure of protection.

Prisoners often establish friendships by teasing one another or calling each other nicknames. Names can be based on the hood that the individual grew up in or a unique personality trait or physical feature. Not only do cons call each other names, but they have some reserved for certain officers, too.

Except in some of the rougher medium and high-security facilities, most of the convicts aren't such bad guys, as long as you avoid the psychotic types. But even the relatively decent fellows won't hesitate to use you if they can do it without much risk to themselves.

Interpreting Your Commitment Papers

Your fellow cons will probably skip the niceties and cut straight to the chase: "What's your conviction?" "What are you doing time for?" or "How much time did you get?" You will probably answer something like "I got 10 years for a drug conspiracy." Your new friend may then ask to see your commitment papers that list the conviction(s) and sentence. Then he may tell you, in a matter of fact tone, that you will only end up doing eight years plus change. This will probably be news to you, as your lawyer never told you how your sentence would be converted into prison time. The fact is, for all their knowledge of the law and court procedure, few attorneys have a clue as to how much time in prison a client will eventually serve on a given sentence. Nevertheless, the convicts will know, almost to the day, the time you must serve before your release.

Prisoners have read many commitment papers, understand how "jail time" and "good time" is deducted, and the recent decisions of the parole board (assuming you are in a state that still has parole and indeterminate sentences). The convicts will decipher your documents, and depending upon the crime, sentence, and how you score on negative indicators (past convictions, violence, narcotics), give you a pretty good idea of how much time you will actually serve in prison.

It may give you some comfort to know that you do not have to do the entire time day-for-day in prison, as the years may be cut by "good time" or parole. On the other hand, it may shock you to learn that your commitment papers contain bad news, like possession of a weapon, violence, or conviction for heroin or crack cocaine, that will dramatically lessen your opportunity for early parole. In any case, you will find out that every cellblock has "jailhouse lawyers" who will give you more truth than your attorney ever dared to share. (In case you were wondering, jailhouse lawyers are looked down upon by prison administrators, because they can file legal briefs for themselves and fellow inmates; it's not unusual for cons well versed in the law to find themselves transferred frequently.)

Avoiding Favors and other Pitfalls

No experienced con gives up something for nothing. Everything has its price, including information. An act as seemingly innocuous as accepting a cigarette from another con may set you on a slippery slope of ever-mounting obligation on your part and ever-increasing demands by the uncharitable giver. Be careful about owing anybody, because you never know when the bill may come due. For new prisoners, the best advice is to do no favors and request none. Don't try to "buddy up" with the other cons too quickly. You don't need friends. You need alliances based on mutual self-interest. Remember, alliances are built on ever-shifting sands, so stay alert to see which way circumstances may change.

Volunteer as little information as possible about yourself and your personal life. Every fact you give out about yourself is a potential handle that someone else might use to manipulate you. Those who confide little run less risk of being betrayed.

Do your own time. Keep to yourself as much as possible, but be sure not to look as if you're afraid of others. Project a cool, quiet aura of self-possessed confidence, and be prepared to back it up with action when needed. The other guy has got to know that if he messes with you, he's going to pay a price. Move quickly and decisively to defend your rights early on, and it'll make the rest of your stay a lot easier.

The beating you give to another con trying to make a move on you may well earn you a few weeks or even months in solitary in the hole, but when you come out it'll work to your advantage among the rest of the prison population. But watch out for the guy you hammered and his clique trying to take revenge.

Prison World, USA, is one predictable destination for many men and women raised in institutions, poverty, or dysfunctional families. Some of your cellmates have grown up living in public housing projects, cheap hotel rooms, or state-subsidized apartments. Many come from single-parent or broken families. Others were raised as wards of the state, in foster homes or orphanages for displaced children, or juvenile detention facilities. They may have had a dozen or so orphan brothers and sisters all growing up together, eating meals at long noisy tables. As state-raised youth they have a vast array of experiences and contacts which, in many respects, may make their stay in prison a lot easier for them and much better than the average middle-class prisoner. These experiences have toughened and prepared them for prison, where stoicism, smarts, and raw nerve are required to persevere and weather hardship and adversity. In many prisons, these state-raised youths are the men who make the rules and run penitentiary cellblocks. These men will show you how to survive and thrive in a concrete jungle.

Part of that survival is understanding the so-called "convict code" and the penalties and dangers that it holds for the unwary. Violations of the unwritten rules vary in severity from disrespectful glances to swift, violent death.

✴ The Convict Code

What follows is the convict code, at least the idealized version cons give lip service to and outwardly endorse:

Do:

Mind your own business

Watch what you say

Be loyal to convicts as a group

Play it cool

Be sharp

Be honorable

Do your own time

Be tough

Be a man

Pay your debts

Don't:

Snitch on another convict

Pressure another convict

Lose your head

Attract attention

Exploit other convicts

Break your word

Like most codes of conduct, this one is not always honored. For example, some guerilla convicts may pressure and exploit each other. In many prisons, organized gangs or cliques of prisoners who've demonstrated a readiness, if not eagerness, to use violence to get what they want may run the rest of the convicts in a cellblock. Here's one area where the convict code's abhorrence of snitching works in favor of the most brutal and vicious exploiters of their fellows. Convicts can beat, rape, even kill their fellow inmates, but one mustn't snitch on them. That wouldn't be honorable to the convict code.

Apart from any scruples you might have about informing, the main reason for not doing so is an eminently practical one: Snitching, no matter the reason for it, may result in a potential death sentence for he who tells tales to the authorities.

In a sense, the informer has shaken hands with the devil. Once you've told tales to the guards, they've got something on you: namely, the knowledge that you are a snitch. Threatening to reveal this to the other cons provides a club with which to beat you into informing again and again, until you're fatally compromised. And if someone finds out and knifes you to death in the showers, well, there's always plenty more snitches to be found.

Generally, convicts practice serious courtesy and careful manners, as this is the only way to avoid offending or insult. An insult that may on the outside be brushed off takes on a deeper meaning in the joint and can be interpreted as fighting words. You must be very careful not to unnecessarily disrespect or "dis" other prisoners. This requires attention to cultural differences and a fair amount of tact. For example, you never enter another man's house (cell), sit on his bed, or touch his personal property without his permission. Never look *too* close at a man's family pictures, or make smart-aleck remarks about his good-looking wife or sister on visiting day. And under no circumstances ever make fun of a man because of his looks, language, lack of formal education, or failure to receive family mail or visits.

The safe way to conduct yourself is to always act as if no convict is better than another. This way you avoid making unnecessary enemies.

The convict's code isn't the only set of rules you'll need to live by in prison—you also must become familiar with the official prison regulations.

Prison Dos and Don'ts

The prison rule book that you received in orientation, which by now you either lost or is tattered, lists the official prisoner dos and don'ts. Some typical dos are that you must *obey a direct order, stand for count, keep your cell orderly,* and *report to work on time.* Included in the list of don'ts are *don't fight, don't have weapons or drugs,* and *don't possess contraband.*

Contraband

The official rule book defines contraband as any item not on your inmate inventory list. All items in your cell or locker must be included on this sheet of paper. Anything found on your person or in your house (your cell) that is not prison issue or purchased from the commissary is considered contraband. This of course includes drugs, alcohol, weapons, coins or paper bills. Generally, no one— not even your family—is allowed to mail you personal possessions; however, books may be mailed to you from publishers.

Most jails and prisons are losing the drug war in their own institutions. Many facilities are flooded with contraband (drugs, alcohol, or weapons). It is common to see convicts smoking pot, snorting cocaine, shooting heroin, or drinking either homemade or commercial liquor. The introduction of illegal drugs or alcohol into prisons is usually attributed to visitors or staff. Convicts, who can be quite innovative, have developed additional schemes to defeat the most sophisticated security, including air drops from flying planes that buzz the prison at night. (By the way, prisons are easy to spot from the air at night because they are all lit up with bright security lights.) Every morning, prisoners check the yard, looking for rubber balls or waterproof packages filled with dope. A less high-tech approach used at many prisons is simply to throw or use sling shots to deliver tennis balls with drugs inside over the wall or fence.

While you may not now indulge in illicit chemical recreation, once you arrive in prison, you may decide to experiment.

Warning: Many men and women with no previous drug experience have become addicted to narcotics while in prison.

Gambling

Although all gambling is against official rules, it is a common practice throughout the prison system—especially sports betting—and it is probably responsible for more institutional violence than drugs or gang affiliation. Convicts' gambling includes card games, dominoes, chess, checkers, dice, and various televised sports events. The most frequent beatings and killings in prison may occur during or after the World Series, NBA playoffs, or NFL Super Bowl.

Common currency in prisons for settling bets is cartons of cigarettes. Large wagers may be paid off through outside bank accounts that are maintained by free-world friends.

Some high roller prisoners place big bets they cannot cover and then pay the price other ways. Nothing in the "convict code" prohibits sticking a shiv (knife) into someone who can't pay a gambling debt. One of the authors of this book remembers doing time in Leavenworth (Kansas) during the World Series between the St. Louis Cardinals and the Kansas City Royals. Convict betting on the games resulted in numerous stabbings and deaths.

Tattoos

One of the first things that outsiders notice about many convicts and ex-cons is their tattoos and distinctive forms of speech. Tattoos done in prison are often rudimentary and done with India ink, ashes from Bible paper, or ink pen refills. A favorite of many prisoners are simple Bic pens where the metal tips are used. More elaborate tattoo rigs are made from Parker pens with cassette player motors taped on the top that serve to move the point up and down.

In most jails and prisons, tattooing is against the rules, and the violator can be punished with a trip to the hole. Tattoo artists receive the respect of their fellow convicts for the sophistication of their work and the risks they take. They usually do fine line tattoo designs that take many hours to complete. Although many prisoners (especially bikers) come into the institutions with tattoos, a greater number leave with fresh artwork.

Shakedowns, Cell Searches, and Extractions

In every joint there are constant staff searches of prisoners. This may happen on the yard, in the corridors, as you're leaving the chow hall, or nearly anywhere. In all penitentiaries there are numerous metal detectors located throughout the prison. You will be ordered to take off your shoes, empty your pockets, and walk through these devices throughout the day. At any time, a guard can order you to stand against the wall to be searched and frisked or waved with a hand-held metal detector, or strip for a full body cavity search. You might even be strip-searched outdoors in the cold and made to stand for hours under the gun towers.

Periodically, your cell is going to get searched for contraband and/or intimidation purposes. Depending on the prison, your cell will be searched once a week or month. A special team of guards dressed in Darth Vader battle dress may enter your cellblock and order everybody out of their houses. Usually, though, the guards "toss" your cell while you are at your workstation (kitchen, factory, mopping halls, etc.). They enter your house and empty the locker on the floor, turn over the bed and throw your personal property into the cell-house corridor. More than likely, they find nothing. Still, you need to review your personal property on a regular basis to make sure no contraband has been planted in your cell.

If the guards are serious about finding drugs, they will turn off the water service in the cell-house, which drains the toilets, preventing convicts from flushing dope. In some joints they use dogs to detect and locate drugs and alcohol. These same canines may be used for perimeter and tracking escaped convicts.

Should you be foolish enough to defy the guards by refusing to come out of your cell when ordered to do so, the officers will get the Special Emergency Response Team (goon squad, according to the cons) together to perform a cell extraction. Once you've been forcefully removed from your cell, you'll get a shot (be written up) and be sent to the hole.

Getting a Shot

If you are caught violating prison rules, you get a shot, also referred to by prisoners as getting written up or issued a ticket. Prison administrators may call them incident or disciplinary reports, but no one else does.

Many court decisions govern disciplinary punishment of prisoners. At the very least, you are entitled to a notice of the charges and a hearing. Once written up, you will be given a disciplinary hearing, in which the hacks escort you into a room with a table. One or more seated officers will read the charges against you, ask you for your response, then pronounce you guilty. Like a kangaroo court, it is your word against theirs, so the outcome is nearly always predictable. Usually, you'll receive a punishment, which may include some loss of privileges. Some common punishments include loss of 30 days' good time, loss of commissary privileges for one year, or 90 days in the hole.

The Hole

If you catch a serious shot and are dragged to the hole, officially called an administrative segregation unit, you will be stripped of your general population uniform and dressed out in segregation clothing. This is usually a jumpsuit—its color will depend upon the joint and the level of solitary confinement; for example, prisoners in protective custody may be dressed in a different color jumpsuit, as compared to a man in disciplinary segregation.

If you raise hell in solitary, the guards may remove all of your clothes and throw you into a strip cell, or they might let you cool your heels in a dark cell with no lights. Continue to act up, and the hacks might tighten the screws by strapping you to a board or a chair with four point restraints. If they really want to get nasty, they can tie you down in a straight jacket and shut you up by either putting a rag in your mouth or putting tape over it.

Enduring Isolation

Now that you're in the hole, whether it's a segregated housing unit, protective custody unit, control unit, or supermax penitentiary, your living conditions will deteriorate. Expect to have limited lighting, usually just one light bulb that stays on all night. It is common to be placed in segregation cells with no clothes, beds, or blankets. The very worst is when the cell is cold or hot, you are naked, and the floor and walls are smeared with human waste.

Locked in the hole, men learn to occupy their time with the most mundane activities. At first you try to pass the time by sleeping, but this only works for the first few days. Next you may study the graffiti, or attempt to converse with inmate orderlies (prisoners who are paid to care for or watch over other prisoners) or even the hacks. Then again, you may have critters in your cell to help endure the monotony. A favorite pastime of convicts is to train cockroaches to race or to adopt mice or baby rats as pets. Such recreational pursuits may keep you busy for a few weeks.

Eventually, despite your best efforts to stay focused, the lack of human interaction will take its toll. As the loneliness becomes unbearable, you will talk to yourself, assume different characters, and carry on terrific conversations. Your mind will begin to wander as you drift into a delusional state, where your thoughts race from place to place as if in a dream or maybe a nightmare. You'll know you've reached a low point when the walls begin to close in on you, making the space ever smaller.

Prisoners who are subjected to long periods in solitary confinement may suffer what psychologists call psychopathological consequences and sensory deprivation stress. Symptoms can include anxiety, hearing noises or voices, seeing ghosts, profound depression, perceptual distortions, hallucinations, and paranoia. Men who have spent many years in segregation are known to crack up and become violently psychotic, lose the ability to talk with others, and experience amnesia—they may not even recall their own names. Women in solitary are reported to have used pins to carve their names on their arms so they don't forget them. For both men and women in long-term solitary, there is a high rate of self-mutilation, head-banging, and suicide.

It pays to have connections—a few good friends who see to your needs while you are in solitary. If you are lucky, another convict will smuggle in to you a pack of smokes, books, and writing materials. The hacks might even ignore this violation of segregation rules if you don't flaunt the contraband, make too much noise, or give them a bad time. If you've got good buddies, they will find a way to continue this support until you are released back to general population.

Administrative Detention

To complicate matters, many prison systems also use what's called administrative detention to circumvent the legal requirements of providing a disciplinary hearing. The warden simply instructs the officers to remove you from general population and has you thrown into the hole or transferred to another prison. You might land in a supermax, high-security facility (e.g., USP Marion or ADX Florence). As long as the move is the result of an administrative decision, as compared to disciplinary punishment, the law allows the warden to house you wherever he decides. Remember, prison staff enjoy relative immunity for their actions.

Suicide Watch

The prison population may include mentally impaired, elderly, or seriously ill prisoners who attempt to end their own lives. In some facilities, cats who are prone to suicide may be placed on special tiers, stripped of their belts and shoelaces, and given extra supervision, meaning that guards in these units do their rounds more frequently. This is not because they have suddenly become compassionate, it's just that they don't want you to die on their shift—that would mean a whole lot of explaining, paperwork, and a possible lawsuit against the institution.

Most facilities assign other prisoners, sometimes called inmate orderlies, to care for the mentally and physically ill. Why? The guards are too busy attending to so-called routine matters to watch these prisoners. These inmate caregivers may be compassionate and generous in the care they deliver. It is not unusual to see prisoners pushing wheelchairs, emptying bed pans, washing other men in the shower, lifting an old con out of bed, or maintaining a bedside presence throughout the night. Prisoners assigned to suicide watch may work 12-hour shifts, with at least one man on duty around the clock, keeping the suicidal con company and preventing, for a time at least, what may be inevitable. In some joints suicidal prisoners are simply locked up in the hole, as a means of protecting prison authorities from legal liability.

Your Rights and Privileges

Prisoners have few rights and privileges. Still, most joints have an inmate library (filled with paperback books), a law library (with a copy machine, typewriter, and legal journals), weight-lifting area (either inside or outside), education unit, yard (for walking and jogging), and screen for an occasional movie. General population prisoners may have access to these areas. These privileges may be revoked for breaking the rules. If you're in the hole, you're not going anywhere.

Personal Belongings

In your cell, you'll have a military-style locker where you store your stuff—books, cigarettes, clothing, and food. It has a combination lock that provides minimal protection from theft by locker knockers, thieving scavengers, or gang bangers who try to steal from these contraptions—steal from *you*, who has to eat out of that locker. (In the long run, they usually end up being badly beaten or even better, dead, if they get caught in a dormitory or cellblock.)

In some state penitentiaries, prisoners are allowed to have their own television and stereo system. Federal prisoners are not allowed to have TVs in their rooms.

Each prison has a number of TV rooms, each with a TV protected by a plastic cover. Only the guards are allowed to change the channels. There may be a few hundred men watching TV at one time, and whenever someone wants to change the channel they take a vote and ask the guard to do it for them. If you don't like the idea of hanging out in a crowded TV room, you can purchase small personal radios in the commissary, like a Walkman. But you must use headphones with them at all times. And you are not allowed to use computers for any reason, so this means that you do not have access to the World Wide Web.

Phone Calls

The prison phone system is complicated. You cannot simply go to any phone and call out. Instead, in some prisons, your case manager must set up your phone account, complete with a short list of the few numbers you are allowed to call. Usually, inmate phones do not have keypads—the prison operator does the dialing for you.

You must tell the operator your name, inmate number, the person you are calling, and the phone number. If the person you intend to call is not on your official list, or their number has changed, you're out of luck. Most state prisons require all calls to be collect, which will eventually drain the family budget. Federal prisoners are required to pay for their own calls out of their commissary account. Either way, the phone calls are very expensive, as much as ten times more than long distance calls on the outside, or more than a dollar a minute.

FBOP prisoners are allowed only 300 minutes of phone time a year, and after 15 minutes, the call is cut off. The time allotted includes the message that is repeatedly played, reminding the callers that the call is coming from a federal correctional facility. The feds believe this practice minimizes criminal activity (e.g., fraud, extortion, and assorted phone scams) which comes from the institution (cons believe such activity is the exception, rather than the rule). For some unfortunate cons, the phone is the only lifeline to their family.

Mail

All prisons have rather rigid rules about mail. First, you must write your family and friends and give them the correct prison address for prisoners. This will include your inmate number and dormitory or cell-house. Second, you must remember that the inmate mail, both outgoing and incoming, is slow, taking as much as a week or longer to arrive. This is because all mail is opened, read, and copied by the staff. Don't bother to have your family or lawyer mail you anything by overnight express.

You will not be allowed any care packages without written permission, and most everything found by staff in letter envelopes will be destroyed without notice to you. If you are mailed any contraband, which includes all items not purchased at the prison commissary, you will be written up. So don't have your mom mail you a new toothbrush, dental floss, stamps, or anything other than the letter. In fact, some prisons limit the number of pages per envelope. For example, in the Missouri Prison system a letter longer than five pages is returned to the sender.

Legal mail from attorneys or the court will be opened in your presence by staff with the date and return name and address logged into some sort of record book. The institution is legally obligated to deliver all official correspondence; besides, they want to know who is making trouble filing lawsuits. If you correspond with the media, expect to get an immediate trip to the hole.

All prisons restrict prisoner access to publications and periodicals. Some will not allow you to receive newspapers, as they claim to have them available in the prison library. Other correctional systems require all books to be mailed only from the publishing companies. The prison may also have a list of banned publications, including sex magazines, dirty books, political magazines, or gang publications. This list may be quite extensive. Expect all books and magazines to be inspected for drugs and weapons, with the covers and spine ripped off by the staff.

Visits by Family and Friends

While some prisoners' wives and girlfriends abandon their spouses and partners and take them to the cleaners, it is also true that when you see a visiting room in most states it is filled with families. They will make the journey to each and every prison their husband, boyfriend, or son is transferred to. Like vagabonds, they may travel with their kids so they can be close to their loved ones who are locked up.

If you're lucky, someone other than your lawyer will visit you while you're in state or federal prison. Who visits you and how they can visit depends upon the type of crimes you were convicted of and on the level of security of the institution you are at. Those incarcerated at supermax facilities rarely are seen by family and friends. The sad fact is that the longer you are incarcerated, the less people visit you, particularly if you are housed far away from where they live and are shifted from one institution to another.

While your family may visit you, and you will be happy to see them, there will be very little physical contact (hugs and kisses). And sex—heterosexual sex, anyway—is not allowed in prison.

Chapter 6

Don't Drop the Soap: Sex in the Slammer

The Number One fear of those going to prison: Being raped. The Number Two fear: Getting killed. Says something about people's priorities, eh? Still, sex has many dimensions that go beyond this primal fear.

Prisons are single-sex institutions, but sex roles in prison are a bit more complicated. In any given facility, there are heterosexuals, homosexuals, transsexuals, and other sexual variations. Without a doubt, there is sex in prison—both consensual and coerced.

Rape in Prison

Sexual assault is not about physical attraction or gratification; it's about violence, politics, power, and business. Some convicts routinely and habitually sexually exploit others. You must always be on guard.

When you're in prison, another convict or group of cons might try to make a move on you, using fear or violence to force you into sexual submission. To surrender will put you at the mercy of violent thugs with a sadistic lust for power and the degradation of the weak, namely those unable to stop them from doing what they want to do. To resist puts you at risk of serious injury (plus you might get raped anyway) or even death.

Those who've been there suggest that, in the long run, if you can handle it, resistance may be the best course. Sexual predators and sadists generally calculate their risk and opportunities and will almost always go for the easy mark rather than the hard target.

The violent understand and respect only violence. You need to make it clear to them that if they attack, you will retaliate. No matter how big or powerful your attackers are, or how many have ganged up against you, you want them to know that you will get even with them when they least expect it. Everybody has to sleep sometime. You may have to inflict serious damage on your foe, without warning, at a place and time of your own choosing. If a group is moving on you, try to arrange things so you can isolate one of your principal tormentors.

If you choose to defend yourself, try to avoid inflicting lethal injury. You don't want to end up facing a murder rap.

Absent a specific, imminent threat, male prisoners get ugly by growing beards, getting tattoos, working out on the weight pile, and assuming a fierce demeanor, all calculated to decrease the likelihood of attack. Just remember: It's all useless window dressing unless it's backed up by the will to inflict sudden, maximum violence on your tormentors.

Homosexuals

Homosexuality is common in the outside free world, so it only stands to reason that gays are also sent to prison. It is estimated that between 3 and 10 percent of the U.S. civilian population is gay. The male prison gay population is probably higher, as some men drift gay or temporarily assume this preference in prison. (We are speaking here of consensual relations, not forced sex.) Convicts are generally more or less tolerant of gays, as long as they keep it to themselves and do not parade their activities in the cellblock. Some gay prisoners get rich in prison by providing sexual services, while others do their time in protective custody or solitary confinement because they are either too popular or have HIV or AIDS.

What happens if a gay convict makes a nonviolent advance on you? It's a rare occurrence. Most real homosexual prisoners have more than enough suitors to choose from. Contrary to popular myth, rarely do they solicit or attack other men. As long as a gay prisoner is quiet about his sexuality and only has a few partners, he is pretty much left alone. Prisoners and staff are amazingly tolerant of this kind of activity, because it helps keep the cons quiet and keeps a lid on things. Some homosexuals even act like they're married, living together and loving each other. They won't walk around holding hands, but most convicts know the situation.

Problems may arise if gays are overly promiscuous or go into business. Homosexual prisoners may be very popular among their crowd, and this can lead to complications. Difficulties can arise, for example, if they start selling sexual favors (hooking) on the yard and cellblock. In some prisons, the hookers can be easily recognized because they wear their pants backward, with the zipper fly on their rear end. Some may even wear makeup and women's clothing to advertise their "femininity." Very often, however, these sexual entrepreneurs are put in solitary because they are constantly hit on and because of the financial implications of their trade. When they go into business, they are quite often successful, and in prison there is not supposed to be any exchange of material items, not even a pack of cigarettes given by one prisoner to another. Prostitution sets up other risky contingencies, too, including jealousy, collecting debts, and extortion (not to mention the spread of sexually transmitted diseases, including HIV).

What happens if the administration places a gay con in your cell? Well, what of it? Mind your own business! It's nothing to you, as long as he takes his action (sex) elsewhere. Most people try to have some privacy in their sexual relations, and your new cellmate should, too. Most homosexual sex goes unseen by all but the participants. However, if your cellmate is gay and he wants to get it on with his buddy in your house, there could be problems. If he proceeds to have sex in your cell and you can't work it out, ask him to request a cell change. If that doesn't work, you may have to ask the guard to move him somewhere else.

All things considered, you may well decide that your cellmate's active sex life is not as bad as sharing the space with a stinking slob, thieving junkie, or violent psychopath. Regardless of sexual preference, the guy who is quiet, keeps to himself, and knows how to do his own time is a good cellmate. Just don't expect gay prisoners to make your bed, do your laundry, or mop the floor three times a day.

Transvestites, Transsexuals, and Transgendered

Your facility may have transsexual prisoners, of which there are two types: pre-op and post-op. The first are biologically male but act female, and the second are men who've been surgically altered (yes, with "the unkindest cut of them all") to one degree or another to biologically resemble a woman. Most transsexuals are pre-op or transgendered men. Most prisoners ignore transvestites and gays, or see them as entertainers who break up the routine boredom of the penitentiary.

Sexual Confusions

Other individuals may drift back and forth, one day dormant, the next taking a walk on the wild side. Their orientation may change as the years pass by behind the wall; deprived of heterosexual affection, they become attracted to their own gender. A heterosexual man may even fall in love and live with another man. In some prisons, especially higher-security prisons for women, love relationships may evolve into pseudo families, with different prisoners assuming the roles of Dad, Mom, and the kiddies.

Heterosexuals

Prisoners adjust to sexual deprivations differently. Many cons just go sexually dormant, putting the thought of having sex out of their mind. In the outside world, most people in the course of their lives have long periods of abstinence, whether that is because of circumstances or choice. In other words, the proclivity to sexual activity is probably more a function of opportunities, relative physical attractiveness, and stage of life. The idea of not having sex as being abnormal is blatantly untrue. People rarely have sex the first or last decade of their life. Often between relationships or marriages, they have periods of celibacy. By some estimates, as much as 10 percent of the population is asexual—they have little interest in sexual activity, and may even live or die as virgins. In other words, it's quite normal to go without sex.

Conjugal Visits

Today, very few prison systems allow conjugal visits. If they are permitted, it is only for prisoners with no disciplinary reports, who are living in minimum security institutions, and are "getting short" (within a year of release). Again, these are token programs, available in few institutions for only a handful of prisoners. Typically, a conjugal visit may last eight hours, one day, or a weekend if it involves family and children. Some prisons still allow furloughs, where you can go home for a couple of days to be with your spouse.

A few correctional facilities for women actually maintain a residence on the grounds where mothers can spend a weekend with their children, but no men are allowed. One prison in the South actually permits prisoners to have conjugal visits where they have sex in cars with their wives, a blanket covering the windshield. Still, most joints have discontinued conjugal visits, so the convicts must make do with what sexual relief they might get breaking visiting room rules. It is not unusual to see prisoners and wives on visiting day sneaking into the public restroom for a quickie.

Everybody Masturbates

Masturbation is fairly common for both men and women, whether they're locked up or in the free world. So most prisoners get some sexual release, and exercise their needs through auto-eroticism. In fact, this may preoccupy a new convict's initial few months in the can, especially if he or she had regular sex on the outside. This activity may be enhanced through using written or visual pornography, although many prisons prohibit the distribution of pornography either because it offends the warden on religious grounds or under the theory that it increases sexual violence and predation. While it may be disturbing to see or hear your cellmate lying on his bunk masturbating, try to have some compassion for him.

Fantasyland?

Some convicts do get lucky and get some hetero sex in the slammer, but most of the time such stories are just that, stories told by other cons to entertain their friends. Cons released on work detail or some other temporary release may get a chance to have "sexual relations" with some ugly broad, like Burt Reynolds's character did in *The Longest Yard*.

On rare occasions a prisoner may get it on with a lady hack or other female staffer. After all, women prison employees are human, and it's not unusual for them to be attracted to bad boys with tattoos and bulging muscles—especially if all they have waiting for them at home is a couch potato whose idea of fun is spending the entire weekend watching pro sports. You've probably figured out by now that all such activities are against prison rules.

Chapter 7

My Baloney Has a First Name: Food in Prison

With taxpayers having to shell out around $15 billion yearly to maintain the prison system, it should come as no surprise that prison food is no gourmet fare and the medical system is bare bones.

My Dog Wouldn't Eat This: Cafeteria Food

Convicts refer to institutional meals as dog food, Kennel Rations, or Alpo. Still, it beats the old days of bread and water. It is typically served in large cafeterias, also called the chow or dining hall. A typical dinner meal in the pen may be brown lettuce, blue fruit, and mystery meat (which is never red). The hamburger will be low quality and the chicken will look like a small pigeon. Many days the food is prepared, served, and thrown out, with only a small number of cons daring a taste. Fear of food poisoning generally beats out hunger.

Cafeterias may serve coffee, tea, soft drinks, or fruit juice. You always get milk, because it's government surplus. Rarely is the food fresh. The only vegetables are canned, wilted lettuce being the exception, and for fruit you get soft bananas and bruised apples. In some joints in the deep South, they serve catfish or fish heads, cornbread, and grits, always grits.

Generally, the best meals are served on holidays. For example, on Thanksgiving or Christmas the kitchen might prepare food of somewhat better quality. It won't be like a home-cooked meal, but you might get mashed potatoes and dressing, sweet potatoes, turkey, or ham.

Some prisons have special dietary food lines for diabetics and other medical prisoners, or kosher meals (a simple diet with no pork) for Jews and Muslims. If the food looks better in the kosher line than the standard fare that is being offered that day, then suddenly a thousand convicts in the institution will appear to have mysteriously converted to Judaism or Islam. Alternatively, if the special-diet food becomes disgusting, only the truly devout will stick to their religio-dietary principles. Regardless of which meal line you join, usually the only food worth eating is the bread, cake, or cookies prepared by convict bakers.

Prisoners who work in the cafeteria generally eat better than the other cons. This explains why they continue to work seven days a week, twelve hours a day, cooking and dishwashing. Many also use this job detail to go into business. Typically, they make grilled cheese sandwiches and hamburgers and sell them in the dormitories and cellblocks. Mess hall workers are also often in the moonshine business (i.e., prison hooch, pruno, or rotgut) because they have access to yeast, sugar, fruits, and vegetables. What's their recipe? Fill a black plastic garbage bag with a combination of the above mentioned materials and hide it somewhere (e.g., inside a toilet or under a bed) while it ferments; it eventually yields a couple of gallons of low-quality alcohol.

In some minimum security facilities, convicts who can afford it will eat their meals out of vending machines. They'll purchase canned franks and beans, chili, and sandwiches. Then they heat it up in a nearby microwave oven. Of course they'll pay top dollar for the privilege of eating this kind of fare. And it's not unheard of for the vending service to be owned by relatives or associates of the warden.

Generally, if you can afford to buy food through commissary (we'll talk about this in a minute), the dining hall is to be avoided. In many joints, the cons with institutional jobs, a racket, or outside money mailed in, either purchase kitchen food or eat commissary items out of their lockers. In some federal prisons, organized crime and drug cartel prisoners may purchase steaks and lobster from the guards. It is common to see well-connected cons eating Pizza Hut or Kentucky Fried Chicken. Depending on the joint, as the food differs from one to another, cons hustle food to stay healthy and avoid illness.

Grocery Shopping, Prison Style

Each prison has what is known as a commissary, which sells basic items to general population prisoners. It's not like a Safeway, Whole Foods Market, or even a 7-11. Depending on the facility, the commissary is open either once a week or month. The prison prints out an order form that is distributed to the convicts, which lists a limited selection of items for sale. These include food, stationery, toiletries, and clothing. In terms of food, the list will contain cheap brands of cookies, crackers, candies, and canned food like tuna, salmon, and sardines. The most common food item purchased by prisoners is tuna. It comes in one of those pull-top cans, making it unnecessary to use a can opener, which you are not allowed to have.

You buy items from a commissary with some idea of how you are going to eat for the week or month and what complements what, like tuna and crackers, or sardines and crackers. You can make nachos, for example, out of jalapeno peppers, tortilla chips, and cheese. As your Hispanic cellmates will tell you, hot peppers clean out your system and protect you from different kinds of sickness that pervade prisons. Because of all the overcrowding and lack of fresh air, prisons are dirty and dusty, and jalapenos seem to help purge your sinuses and digestive tract.

The commissary is typically run by an officer who has a couple of prisoners working for him. It's not like a typical walk-in grocery in the free world. You stand in a very long line leading up to a glass or screen window, in front of a counter like you'll find in most banks. The commissary has the feel of those hardened security convenience stores attached to gas stations in crime-ridden neighborhoods. This prison store is usually located in a hallway, and the guards call cons down by cellblocks, sometimes 500 guys at a time. You might have to wait in line for a couple of hours. But what the hell, you're not going anywhere else anyway.

When you're in a commissary line, you're vulnerable. You are physically exposed, a stationary target. If you owe someone money, it's a perfect time for the creditor to demand his money or stab you in the heart. In prison, debt-collecting and murder are often one and the same thing. For this reason, it's not unusual for debtors and institutional snitches to pass on commissary altogether.

Each prisoner in line fills out his commissary list, which is a two-sided piece of paper with all the prices of the available items. You check off what you want, add everything up, put your name and inmate number on the front of it, and then present your ID or commissary card (which may be one and the same thing) at the window.

A commissary ID is like a credit card with your picture on it. If you lose your card, misplace your list, add up the prices incorrectly, or don't have enough money in your account, you're out of luck. In most joints, you can't go back to your cell to find your card or list, drop out of the line to go to the bathroom, or have someone hold your place. Jump the line, and sooner or later you're going to get hurt or killed.

When you come to the commissary window, you hand the officer your list, and the inmate workers fill a paper bag with what you have requested. Remember, commissary is a privilege—not a right—and in prison "the customer is never right." If you added your items up wrong, the guard might rip up your request. Change your mind at the last minute, and he may deny you commissary that week or month. If you cause a fuss, it may be enough to irk the guard to tell you to move on. Give the officer any back talk, he may order you back to your housing unit without filling your order.

Here's another scenario. You make 20 bucks a month. You got it all worked out what you're going to buy and what it's going to cost you, but your calculations are off by a few cents and you don't have enough money. That's enough for a correctional officer to forego giving you commissary that time. Hacks have little patience for sloppy arithmetic or bad attitudes.

How do you get money placed in your commissary account? One way is for outsiders to mail you a postal money order. The officers, when they inspect the mail, are supposed to take it out and place it in your name on the books. Alternatively, the meager amount of money you make, your pay, gets placed in the account.

Why does this system exist? Part of the reason is that you're not allowed to carry any dollar bills or coins in most prisons. The administration doesn't want you to have any money to use if you escape. Nor are you allowed any kind of jewelry except for a watch—a cheap one, which you can purchase in the commissary.

Prison administrators never tell convicts how much money they have in their account. Nor are the officers going to tell you. You're supposed to keep track of it. They don't maintain a system like a bank, which mails you a monthly statement, nor are there any ATM machines for easy access. If your commissary list adds up to more than what is available in your account, you're out of luck. Now, if you're a reasonable guy, have worked for and/or been respectful to the guard who is responsible for commissary that day, he may tell you that you are 10 cents off. But say something rude to the officer or give him a dirty look, and he'll tear up the sheet.

Convicts will talk about "making commissary," which simply means that they have the opportunity that week or month to go to commissary. This also depends on having money available on account, and being free at the appointed time. Remember, commissary is only open for your cellblock for a couple of hours, say Wednesday from 3–5 P.M. If, for example, you are in the visiting room, working in the factory, or have some appointment with your case manager in his office, you'll miss commissary. Or, you may be in the last part of the line and five o'clock rolls around. You're out of luck, because commissary closes at five o'clock sharp.

You should keep the amount of funds in your commissary account secret, to protect yourself from predatory inmates. If other prisoners know how much you've accumulated, they may try to borrow from you, sell you drugs, attempt to get you involved in their gambling schemes, or muscle you to extort funds. If you have welshed on a loan or owe someone some money for drugs or a gambling debt, you're already in deep trouble. If word gets out about how much money you have in your commissary account, you may be more readily victimized.

One of the biggest prisoner complaints about the system is that commissaries make a lot of money. The prices are inflated and they don't have to pay any taxes. Essentially, the prison operates a legal monopoly.

One thing you might look forward to with commissary is buying a number of pints of ice cream. It won't be gourmet fare, but they may offer a choice of basic vanilla, chocolate, or Neapolitan and then (since you don't have access to a refrigerator) you immediately share the extra with your friends. Some of your buddies may not have commissary, so this may help lift their spirits, not to mention binding them to you in the web of obligations and alliances so necessary to survive and thrive in the joint.

Eating out of Your Locker

Money aside, how do you determine what you will buy from commissary and keep in your locker? You look at the menu for the week or month, which is posted outside the chow hall, and determine which meals you are going to try or avoid. You buy enough food to cover the cafeteria meals you plan to skip, and store it in your locker. In short, this scenario should convince you that it costs money to live in prison. Most estimates suggest that you need about $100 a month to go to commissary, and more if you smoke.

Most prisoners keep instant coffee or tea—which, like everything else, they buy from commissary—in their locker. Provided the dormitory or cellblock has hot water, you can prepare hot drinks, even soup, in coffee cups. Some lower-security institutions may even provide microwave ovens for the use of prisoners to heat up commissary or vending machine items. The prison administrators are happy to have you pay for your own food.

The only food you can officially have in your locker are the items purchased at commissary. If you have any kitchen food in your locker, including hamburgers that you bought from a kitchen staffer or stuff you brought from the dining hall, you go to the hole. Guards get more upset over cons making alcohol than smoking pot. If you are caught with yeast or sugar, components for hooch, you get locked down in segregation. The reason is apparent if you have ever seen an entire cellblock drunk on homemade brew. Drunken convicts are a dangerous group. They may assault each other or the guards, or damage institutional property. At the very least, they will raise hell and make a lot of noise.

Mind you, the previously described situation is for the general prison population. If you're in the hole, you get no commissary. In addition to losing your freedom, commissary is the first privilege that is taken away from you. You can lose commissary for a variety of infractions, including carrying a shank (which typically results in a year without commissary), messing up the count (being out of place when the officers count the prisoners), or refusing a direct order.

Some people are under the misconception that if you are overweight, being incarcerated will help you shed those extra pounds. But it's not unusual to see fat people remain heavy because of all the bad food available. Mostly, the food convicts eat (whether from the cafeteria or commissary) contains a considerable amount of sugar and starch; it has very little high-quality protein and there are almost no low-fat foods (e.g., juice or fish). Unless you exercise a lot (walking, running, and lifting weights), you are probably going to put on weight.

Catching an Illness, Getting Sick, and Dying

When you go to prison, you have to worry about catching a serious disease and ending up dead. Jails and prisons are notoriously unhealthy places, and prisoners can develop any number of illnesses. Years ago, convicts routinely contracted Cholera, Yellow Fever, and Tuberculosis (TB). This is probably why TB used to be called "jail cough" or "prison fever." Prisons are typically dirty and overcrowded, lack proper sanitary conditions, and have foul air. In situations like this, any communicable disease can quickly spread through the entire population. Diseases are usually transmitted via air or through bodily fluids, like semen, blood, and saliva.

In prison, unlike the army, there is no health education. No one warns you about diseases and how to protect yourself. In most facilities condoms are contraband. No posters or memos about how to protect oneself from AIDS or other scourges grace the walls. Certainly, the prison staff has information, training, and equipment for protecting themselves. (Prison guards now wear plastic gloves not only when they are cleaning up blood, but when they are physically handling a prisoner.)

Tuberculosis and Hepatitis

TB is spread in places that are overcrowded and have dirty, stale, and stagnant air. Let's say there's someone on your tier who coughs and hacks a lot. You're worried that he might have TB. There's very little you can do about it, because you're locked up together. Although prisoners routinely have TB tests, if you have an adverse reaction to it (red marks on your skin), you might be told not to worry about it. If in fact you test positive for these tests, it is pretty much kept a secret, because the prison authorities don't want you to be attacked by fearful prisoners.

Hepatitis, a disease of the liver, is spread through blood, semen, bad water, or spoiled meat. In the early stages you may not know you have it. As the illness progresses, your eyes and skin turn yellow (with jaundice). It will make you very tired, and if not treated quickly, it may lead to death. Many people from developing countries, alcoholics, junkies, and intravenous drug users have hepatitis.

Having any of these diseases is confidential information. If there is an outbreak, the prison medical staff may not take the time to do the appropriate tests to isolate the disease.

AIDS (Another Type of Life Sentence) ✗

As you probably know, you don't have to be gay to get AIDS. Many of the people sentenced to a correctional facility are drug addicts or heavy intravenous drug users, and it goes without saying that AIDS is high amongst this population. What does this all mean? If you do continue your dangerous habit behind bars, then you need to take extra-special precautions, including sterilizing your instruments (which are, as you suspected, contraband). Because of the health risks, your trip to the joint may be a good time to get clean.

Another note of caution: When someone is poked or stabbed, there is usually a lot of blood on the floor and on the walls. Avoid coming into contact with the blood at all costs, as it could carry any number of infectious organisms, including the virus that causes AIDS.

Good Luck Staying Healthy

Many prisoners spend a lot of time worrying about and doing things to maintain their health. Physical assault aside, prison life presents a number of serious challenges to a person concerned with avoiding illness or medical injury.

Prisons are noisy places, with slamming of cell doors, a lot of screaming and yelling, and a constant racket that reverberates off the cement and steel. The noise will remind you of a crowded bus station or shopping center, where the background drone of hundreds of voices may drown out your own voice. The noise is so bad that some prisons actually use soundproof audio booths and headphones to clinically test convicts for hearing damage. There is little you can do to protect yourself from hearing loss, as there is no way to avoid the pandemonium inside the cellblocks—except to cover your head with a pillow or take every opportunity available to be outside in the yard, where the sound dissipates in the open air.

And then there's the food, which as noted earlier is deplorable. The best advice we can offer is to limit your exposure to food poisoning by skipping cafeteria meals that appear risky and supplement your diet with commissary food, vitamins, and a lot of liquids to flush your system. A common precaution used by prisoners to protect themselves from bacterial infection is to wash their hands frequently and eat liberal amounts of hot peppers and salsa. This also works to clear your nasal passages and sinuses, and may help with cold symptoms and allergies.

If you do get sick, it's important to make sure you are not issued the wrong medication or even placeboes. One of the authors remembers convicts who were pharmacists before their convictions, standing watch over the med line every morning at sick call and inspecting the prescribed medication provided to prisoners, making sure they were given the right pills.

When you do get sick, pray it is nothing serious, as the medical services are limited and substandard, nothing like the care and attention you have come to expect in the free world. Prisoners suffering from chronic or acute illness will find medical staff to be few, overburdened, and even if they care to help, prevented from doing so by a prison healthcare system that is under-funded, bureaucratic, and severely limited in the services and medical procedures authorized. Most prisoners will tell you that if you need surgery, expensive medication, or sophisticated medical protocols, you need to have family and friends to pressure prison administrators. A life-threatening illness—for example, cancer, heart attack, or stroke—will require outside intervention, possibly a lawsuit or a letter or phone call from a powerful politician, to get you transported to a civilian hospital.

Many prisons now have geriatric cellblocks filled with elderly prisoners, many of them in wheelchairs, on respirators, or in beds hooked up to machines or intravenous tubes feeding fluids and medicine. The graying of the prison population continues unabated, with more convicts serving life sentences and expiring behind the wall. Some prison systems allow elderly prisoners, or younger convicts diagnosed to die in a few months, to apply for compassionate release. This may allow the person to go home and die in the company of his loved ones. The problem is, few prisoners ever make it out the door before they pass away, as the application process may take many months to officially approve.

The best way to maintain or even improve your health is daily exercise, at least walking the yard, possibly jogging, lifting weights, or playing sports like basketball, handball, or softball. Yes, some minimum security camps may have one tennis court, but you will have to wait in a long line to use it.

The good news is, despite the poor food and inadequate medical services, many prisoners do use exercise, especially long walks, to work off stress, lose weight, and improve their health. Some men overcome their addictions to alcohol and drugs, establish a daily routine of exercise, and leave prison in better health than when they entered it.

Can I Bum a Smoke?

Prisons sell tobacco products in commissary. Like in the military, the prices for smokes in federal joints are lower than on the street because there is no markup for federal taxes. Many prisoners smoke, if only to live up to the tough-guy image they try to create. Until recently, prisoners were allowed to use cigarettes, cigars, and chewing tobacco nearly everywhere. Jail and prison cellblocks were typically littered with cigarette butts, and heavy smoke filled the air.

The past few years have brought a dramatic change in the rules concerning the use of tobacco products in the nation's jails and prisons. Prison administrators, to avoid potential lawsuits, have banned cigarettes and cigars from interior areas of jails and prisons. Today, most detention facilities strictly forbid both staff and prisoners from lighting up inside. All smokers are now required to take their habit outdoors. Some prisons may even have sheltered designated smoking areas on the yard. A crowd of prisoners usually occupies these areas.

While nonsmokers, and smokers attempting to quit, may welcome these new institutional rules, many smokers complain bitterly about the change. For cons with serious nicotine addictions, being locked in a smoke-free environment all day and night, except for the few hours they are allowed to be on the yard, can be the stiffest part of their sentence.

Maybe knowing the new prison restrictions on smoking will motivate some guys to give up crime and avoid incarceration—or at least give up smoking.

Chapter 8

License Plates and GEDs: Work and School in Prison

Today's prisons are about incarceration, not rehabilitation. A generation ago, some effort was made to rehabilitate convicts in anticipation of their eventual release into the outside world. A quarter-century of high recidivism rates, or habitual criminal behavior, of most career criminals has put this approach in disfavor with authorities, politicians, and taxpayers. Today's emphasis is on protecting the public by locking up criminals and ensuring that they serve most, if not all, of their sentences.

Prison is prison, not high school or college, and opportunities for receiving some form of formal education are in short supply, and getting shorter. Most convicts are lucky to receive basic instruction that would lead to the achievement of GED (General Education Development certificate, basically a high school diploma).

Good jobs in prison (such as they are) are also in short supply. Getting a decent assignment and avoiding bad work details is important for maintaining your morale and earning some meager inmate wages to place in your commissary account. Generally, those prisoners who can type well, or have a college degree, eventually secure positions as inmate clerks.

Prisoners do more than make license plates and mail bags. Prison industries are a vital part of our national economy, producing thousands of different products and providing services marketed all over the country. These include office furniture, clothing, shoes, paintbrushes, and electronic parts. Convicts may work as telemarketers and serve as customer service representatives for banking and credit card services, airlines and hotels, and state lotteries. Next time you receive one of those annoying phone calls from some stranger trying to sell you home repairs or improvements, home equity loans, or vacation packages, it may be a convict on the other end of the line.

Work Details

Not everybody in prison has a job. There are never enough work assignments for the whole population. Some guys spend the whole day in their cells, venturing forth only to go to the library or participate in some sort of recreational activity, such as weight lifting or playing handball. In an institution of about 2,000 prisoners, 400 (20 percent) of the convicts work in the prison industries (factory), 100 (5 percent) cook and clean in the kitchen, another 100 mop floors, another 100 do maintenance work (plumbing, carpentry, air-conditioning repair, painting) and groundskeeping (cutting grass, planting flowers, shoveling snow), 200 (10 percent) are in GED classes, 50 (2.5 percent) are in drug treatment class, 200 are in the hole (usually 10 percent of the prison population can be found in the hole at any one time), and 200 are on medical leave, laid up in their cells or the infirmary with diabetes, heart problems, bad backs, etc. The rest of them—over 30 percent of the prison population—are confined to their housing units, bored out of their minds.

In order for the facility to function properly, convicts must do menial labor. They may work in the kitchen preparing meals, or spend years mopping and waxing corridor floors, or in the laundry cleaning massive amounts of clothing.

The most common job is sweeping, mopping, and waxing floors. The cell-house may be filthy, but the administrative corridors will be spotless, with 20 men running buffer machines day and night, so you'll be able to see your face shining up from the floors. Generally, all the areas of the prison where the public may enter or the brass have offices are cleaned relentlessly. As you move to the interior of the prison, behind the security gates, and into the cellblocks where the prisoners live jammed together, the hallways get dim and dirty.

Inmate Pay

Just because you have a work assignment doesn't mean you'll be paid. Prisons are under no obligation to compensate you for your labor. In fact, many correctional facilities don't pay their inmates anything. When prisons do pay cons, they only pay enough so guys can purchase small items from commissary or cover the cost of their telephone calls. If no cons have money in their commissary account, the place gets really desperate.

The waiting list to get a job in prison industries is usually a couple of years long, because that's the best way to make money. In any event, inmate pay for general labor is very low, a few dollars a week. Mopping floors pays about 12 cents an hour, and working in the factory ranges from about 40 cents to $1.10. Remember—to the authorities, work for convicts is a privilege, not a right. In the outside world, you must work or starve. In prison, you work to keep from dying of boredom.

Vocational Training

Vocational training generally means kitchen, maintenance work, or groundskeeping, which is supervised by guards who provide little instruction to the inmates. Although these are officially called vocational programs, the convicts know they are really work assignments. Unless you are "physically or mentally challenged" (mentally ill, mentally retarded), washing dishes 12 hours a day, 7 days a week can hardly be called vocational training; it will not lead to a better job on the outside.

Hitting the Books

The education programs are always inadequate. Prisons are filled with men and women who desperately need to upgrade their formal education. In some joints a majority of the men are high school dropouts. While we know that this lack of education may have contributed to their attraction to crime, the prison education curriculum will do little to alleviate this problem. Unfortunately, very little resources, staff, and space are devoted to so-called "inmate education."

Typically, a prison will have an education section or department that occupies a floor or wing of a building. This might consist of a small library and a few classrooms and be staffed by a few hacks and a number of convict clerks. In another correctional facility, there may be an education department managed by certified teachers who come into the prison every day and are devoted to the educational success of their convict students. The success of the program depends as much on the determination of the individual prisoners as on the skills of the officer or teachers.

Most maximum or supermax prisons' educational programs are limited to Adult Basic Education (ABE 8th grade), and the GED. The "teachers" may be guards with no training in education.

In every prison there are a dedicated group of prisoners, many of them college-educated, some of them former teachers, who tutor other men for their ABE or GED. FBOP policy emphasizes the need for prisoners to complete these basic requirements.

The only institutional program worth taking may be a 10 month, 8 hour per day, computer repair course, offered on contract by an outside corporation. You may enjoy learning about computer architecture and program languages, but spend most of your time teaching remedial math classes to fellow convicts. Some of them may actually learn enough basic algebra to pass the computer course exams. Unfortunately, this unique prison program is often discontinued when the funding expires.

We suggest that you use your prison time to further your formal education or at least read some good books. While going to prison may cause one to lose spouse and family, many guys still have their health and a strong mind. They need to bury the past and invent new dreams. Some have a GED or even a few years of college already under their belt. They may enter prison determined to somehow complete that degree.

Reading Behind Bars

In the joint, you'll have more free time to read than you've ever had in your life. You may become preoccupied with reading. In the penitentiary, you don't have access to university or public libraries, so you'll need to ask friends to order books from publishers for you; or you can always sift through the worn, tattered, and outdated collection of paperback books in the prison library.

You might consider asking friends to order you classical literature, college textbooks, and political theory. In each prison you might make frequent visits to the library, looking for something worth reading. Even amid volumes of so-called trashy fiction, you can always find a few gems. You may enjoy the works of celebrated authors who've spent time in prison, such as Cervantes, Sade, Hugo, Dumas, Dostoevsky, Solzhenitsyn, O. Henry, Hammett, Genet, Malcolm X, Burroughs (William, not Edgar Rice, who's also good), Himes, Hunt, and Liddy, to name a few. For entertainment, you can't go wrong with such veteran wordsmiths as Stephen King,

Louis L'Amour, Donald Goines, Tom Clancy, Clive Cussler, James Ellroy, Elmore Leonard, Andrew Vachss, Stephen Hunter, Robert A. Heinlein, and anything ever written by Mickey Spillane.

If you're planning to return to university upon eventual release, you can brush up on the physical and social sciences by reading the (admittedly outdated) textbooks found in prison libraries. This allows you an opportunity to get reacquainted with chemistry, biology, geography, and physics. Try some of Isaac Asimov's science primers (you might also enjoy his science fiction). Carl Sagan's *Cosmos* and other books on astronomy allow you to see beyond the narrow confines of your daily existence. Living in prison, locked up at night, with rarely a view of the night sky, you miss the stars.

For political types, there's Machiavelli, Marx, Paine, Burke, Rousseau, Carlyle, Russell, Rand, Chomsky, E.Q. Wilson, Samuel Huntington, and many others.

Other convicts, however, may be more inclined to take their inspiration from Hitler's *Mein Kampf* or the racist propaganda of *The Turner Diaries*.

When Your Teacher's a Con, Too

Semi-formal classes are sometimes organized by prisoners on a wide range of topics. Many of these are taught by men convicted of white-collar offenses or tax crimes and typically cover entrepreneurial subjects like writing business plans, applying for small business loans, and operating a limousine service.

One third of the population in FBOPs is foreign, with prisoners from all over the world. It's relatively easy to find a tutor to help you learn a foreign language, including Spanish—taught by Colombians and Mexicans—and German and French. Also worth noting are the generous instructions by jailhouse lawyers in writing administrative remedies, writs, motions to court, appeals, and post-convict motions. Such free classes taught by convict volunteers are unofficial, with no assistance from prison authorities. Formal classes, beyond GED, with rare exceptions, are not available.

Cons in College

A mountain of academic research clearly demonstrates that higher education is the single most effective means to lower criminal recidivism rates. Simply stated, prisoners who complete a year or more of college courses while incarcerated are far less likely to violate parole or be returned to prison on a new conviction. Still, most prison systems have no post-secondary education offerings at all.

Occasionally, a local college might offer one or two intro level courses, but these are few and far between, dependent as they are upon the institution and the whims of the warden. In any event, they only serve a few dozen prisoners at a time who can somehow scrounge up the funds to pay the tuition. The college may pull the plug on the program when they discover the convicts can't afford the courses and/or when they lose patience with the bureaucrats who manage the penitentiary.

Prison administrators, despite their program propaganda, usually don't actively support higher education. They're jailers, not educators. Most wardens, even those who publicly portray themselves as dedicated to rehabilitation, see outside university instructors as potentially subversive threats to the security and smooth running of the institution.

Convicts taking college classes also may be subject to frequent cell shakedowns and disciplinary transfers to administrative detention (solitary confinement) or other institutions. Wardens may consider educated convicts to be a threat to their authority, because they have the ability to write letters to the media to report inhumane conditions and corruption. Convict students also may be regarded as dangerous because they use the mail and phones to communicate with outside university personnel and other people who have influence with the press or political system.

Goodbye, Pell Grants

Prior to 1992, prisoners could apply for Federal Pell grants, which paid college tuition for courses taught inside prison walls or by correspondence. Some convicts were able to access this program, receive funding, and pay for college credits. Filling out the applications was always a hassle, particularly for federal prisoners, who were more likely to get transferred and thus have to reapply several times. Prisoners no longer have to worry about the hassle, because the grants aren't available anymore.

College Credit by Correspondence

It's a struggle completing college credit by correspondence. Of course, just doing time in prison is a struggle. Nevertheless, every joint has a small group of men who take classes by mail. Typically, they're subject to a number of security restrictions that complicate their efforts, including limitations on the number of books allowed in cells (five), limited access to typewriters or photocopy machines, and restrictive mail procedures. All mail, coming and going, is opened, read, and copied by guards. Books mailed to convicts have the covers ripped off by prison employees, to prevent the entry of contraband into the institution. (The staff is concerned about drugs (sheets of LSD, heroin, or cocaine), weapons (razor or hacksaw blades), or money being hidden in the cloth or paper cover.)

If you're lucky, you may be able to get yourself a position as a clerk in one of the prison factories and can be one of the highest-paid convicts in the facility. You can then use part of your pay to finance college courses by mail. Every month, after making commissary purchases, you might set aside enough to pay for the next course. This process can take you two years to complete five courses (15 credits), and finish the degree requirements for a university semester.

A Guide to University Credit for Prisoners

University study is the single best means to post-prison success. A prison record and a GED provide ex-cons with few prospects other than minimum wage jobs. Cons who complete university credit courses while incarcerated may continue on and finish college degrees at universities when they return home to their communities, thus giving them something to look forward to.

When considering pursuing a college degree, you need to be honest with yourself about your educational background. How far did you get in school? Did you finish high school? Do you like to read and write? Maybe you already started college before being imprisoned. Do you have the ability and determination to do college level studies? You need to make some initial determination, some guess, as to how serious you are about college study.

If you think you're really up to the task, call or have a free-world friend call the University of Wisconsin–Madison Extension (phone 606-262-1748), Ohio University (phone 614-593-1000), or University of Colorado (phone 1-800-331-2801), all of which have excellent university credit programs by mail.

UW–Extension operates one of the best credit by correspondence programs in the country. Ohio University has a "Program for the Incarcerated," which specializes in the needs of prisoners. All three universities have excellent academic reputations, and their credits will transfer without problems to nearly any college in the country. Simply call the phone numbers provided and ask about college credit by mail. Give the university representative your name, prisoner number, and address, and ask him or her to mail the free course catalogue for university credit by mail.

When you receive the catalogue in the mail, read it carefully from cover to cover, making notes about costs, courses you want to take, and university rules and regulations. Most of these university correspondence programs have no admission requirements, and you do not need a GED or high school diploma to begin classes.

You'll have to figure out how to pay for the college credit courses and what courses to take. We suggest you either ask for outside help (family or friends), or work at prison industries to pay for courses. You may have alternative means, for example, doing legal work for others, or other revenue-producing activities. Next, you need to have the prison case manager, counselor, or a free-world friend arrange to issue a money order to be mailed to the university. You could also ask outside family or friends to pay for the first course, and then reimburse them later, over a number of months, or when you get out of prison.

Get started by taking only one course, something you find personally interesting; for example, corrections, criminology, African-American history, Spanish (lots of help available from other prisoners), astronomy or geography (provides intellectual vacation from prison), sociology or anthropology (prison is a great place to study human culture and behavior).

Upon selecting and paying for one course, you will receive a large package in the mail containing the class requirements and assignment sheets to be mailed back to the university. Assignments (usually essays) are reviewed and graded by professors or graduate students. You may need to arrange for the Prison Education Officer to supervise the taking of exams. If you get in over your head, ask for help from other prisoners who are college graduates.

Keep in mind that most prisons have a small number of prisoners taking college credit by mail. They usually hang out in the main prison library or law library, where it is quiet, and they might have access to typewriters and copy machines. Determined prisoners can complete as many as 3–9 credits in 90 days, depending on their funds to pay for courses and stamps, scholastic ability, the conditions of confinement, and their ability to get along with other prisoners and staff.

College credit courses are not for everybody. Prisoners, just like first-year students on college campuses, have a high rate of failure. The good news is that, ironically, prisons are an ideal place to begin college study. You have lots of time to read, room and board is provided, and for the committed student there are few distractions. By beginning college in prison on your own initiative, you're planning a new future, to reinvent yourself and reach for freedom.

Upon release from prison, one possible path you can take is to finish your degree. Your college transcript will help you to gain admission to a university to finish the degree. As a former prisoner, you're already institutionalized, familiar with dormitory living and bureaucratic rules. Besides, considering that you probably don't have a job and so have no income, and haven't paid taxes in years, you'll qualify for generous student loans (which you'll have to pay back ten years after you leave school) and possible grants (free money). Ex-convicts make good students. They're serious learners and masters at overcoming adversity.

Chapter 9

Blood In, Blood Out: Prison Gangs and Violence

Short of being raped, the second greatest fear of prisoners is being beaten, stabbed, or killed in the joint. The higher the security level, the longer the sentences served, the more potential for violence. The most violent convicts are young men serving long sentences. Older prisoners may be more dangerous, but they're more logical in their use of violence. That's why they've survived long enough to become older prisoners.

Teenagers are more inclined than grown men to have fist fights. In prison, altercations don't stay restricted to fists and feet for too long, though. Lead pipes and homemade weapons tend to come in during return bouts. Older men rarely have these sorts of altercations because when they do fight, they often kill each other. Some of it has to do with the fact that as you age, you accumulate more body weight. When you hit someone, (if you're lucky), you'll probably lay them out. More important is the value of experience. When older cons rumble, they're more likely to play for keeps.

Violence is often the currency of crime; fear and intimidation its small change. Psychological and physical violence abound in correctional settings. The first affects the convicts' mental state and leads to cynicism, anger, depression, and resistance to authority—all of which many individuals already had in abundance before ever seeing the inside of a prison cell. Physical violence affects the prisoner's body and, eventually, his mind.

Some of the physical violence is planned, where the con carefully plots out (often in great detail) what he is going to do to a fellow prisoner or a guard. Prison is a great place for holding and acting upon grudges. Most violence, however, is spontaneous, the result of some annoyance or irritation. And there are plenty of things to get bothered about in prison, including crowding, idleness, the food, and the strange behavior of other men. People are on edge, stressed out, and anybody can go off on you at any time.

٠ The annoyance may start when someone steps in front of you in a long line. It's more than a bother, it's a challenge. The line-jumper believes or wants to find out if you can be intimidated. If he gets away with it, he'll be back another time, perhaps upping the ante. So, when he jumps your line, you call him on it, which turns into a shouting match, then some pushing, or a fight.

Guards (and administrators) need to keep a close eye on all forms of violence so they can respond appropriately. If they overreact, like instituting a 24-hour lockdown, or throw too many guys in the hole, they may have a riot on their hands. They also have to provide opportunities for cons to blow off steam, like yard time or access to the gym or library. They don't like it when cons beat the hell out of each other or kill each other, because it generates onerous paperwork that they'd just as soon not bother with. Some guards, though, have been known to instigate violence—for example, by putting two cons who hate each other together in the same cell and sitting back to watch the fireworks.

Disturbances, Rebellions, and Riots

Jails and prisons have experienced their share of disturbances, rebellions, and riots. These are common occurrences and result in a great deal of blood being spilled, usually convict blood.

Disturbances

Disturbances are low-intensity acts of resistance. Usually a disturbance starts with some altercation—a table in the chow hall gets flipped over, or someone damages institutional property in an outbreak of frustration and anger. If the food in the dining hall is particularly vile that day, say, the cons will fill up their trays and simultaneously throw them on the floor. It results in a big mess, which the kitchen workers clean up with shovels. It's not like it's an insult to the chef. The cons who cooked it don't care whether you eat the food or throw it on the floor.

A disturbance may start with one con damaging a chair, and then suddenly 50 guys are doing the same thing. Often, there may be no overt reason for the outburst. And there is no sanctity to the actions. Cons will destroy a dining hall, turn over a delivery truck on the prison grounds, trash a chapel, or trample a bed of newly planted flowers, which were put there by the cons at the express order of the warden. It's a sign of resistance—that they are not totally beaten and still have some fight left in them.

Most disturbances involve a lot of noise. Sound reverberates in cellblocks made entirely of cement and steel. Like in Hollywood films, when the prisoners are unhappy, they make noise by pounding on metal doors or banisters, or screaming profanities at guards. Some cons aren't shy about sliming the guards (throwing human waste at them), either.

With 200 convicts yelling "Fuck you!" what's an officer to do? They can't put the whole cellblock in the hole, but they can take away the rec yard, the weekly movie, or the commissary privileges, which only enrages the cons that much more. Nevertheless, locking down the cellblock and taking away privileges is a frequent occurrence in most prisons in the United States.

Rebellions

Rebellions include work and hunger strikes. When they engage in a work strike, convicts refuse to come out of their cells, go to the factory, cook, or clean the place. Without prison labor, wardens can't effectively and efficiently run the correctional facility. Guards try to identify and round up the ringleaders, often with the help of prison snitches. They'll throw the troublemakers in the hole to cool off until they can be shipped off to a supermax prison.

Work strikes usually end when cons get hungry and run out of food in their lockers. So the prison, much like any other big corporation with striking workers, typically waits out the cons. Strikes don't usually last more than a week or two.

A common form of protest in prisons, especially for political types, is the hunger strike. Although the guards pretty much don't give a damn if a convict starves to death, the situation (especially if the media gets involved) embarrasses the prison authorities. The protest action can also disrupt the orderly running of the institution and irritate—and sometimes even infuriate—the warden.

Riots

When a riot is coming, you can feel it in your bones. Prisoners who've been through them before are more skilled at surviving the next one. Riots aren't just about guards or workers getting injured or killed; they're often opportunities for prisoners to settle old debts. In most riots, more convicts than guards get killed.

Prison riots are doomed to fail. No matter how many guards are taken hostage, beaten, or killed, the uprising will inevitably be crushed with overwhelming force. Those guards who survive, or their replacements, will have months if not years to exact a full measure of revenge on those who've defied them. Payback can be true hell.

Notorious riots include those at New York State Penitentiary at Attica in 1971, New Mexico State Prison at Santa Fe in 1980, and the Ohio Correctional facility Lucasville Prison in 1993. Attica resulted in 43 dead, including 11 prison employees. Santa Fe left 33 dead prisoners, most killed by other cons in an orgy of sadistic brutality that featured murder by blowtorch, decapitation, and dismemberment, as well as beaten guards being gang-raped and then sodomized with nightsticks and lead pipes. The Lucasville riot resulted in 10 dead. Each of these riots included serious injuries to hundreds of prisoners, additional time added to sentences, and tens of millions of dollars of damage to penal institutions. When all is said and done, and the riot is put down, life becomes tougher for the surviving prisoners.

Sometimes riots begin when cliques or gangs decide to settle scores by attacking their rivals. Other reasons include race hatred and battles for prison dominance. Conditions of confinement, such as no heat or air-conditioning in the cellblock, staff abuse of prisoners, and overcrowding may be so oppressive that the cons feel they have no other choice than to hit back hard.

When you riot, you take over the cellblock, part of the prison, or the whole institution. Convicts know that even though they can take control of some or even all of the facility on any given day, they can't hold it for long. The officers will eventually be supported by state police, the national guard, or other military reinforcements. The prisoners may temporarily win the battle but, ultimately, they won't win the war. The authorities will do what's needed to retake the prison, including using tear gas, shotguns, and automatic weapons. But prison riots aren't about any grand strategy or even logic, they're about sticking it to the man (guards, warden, the criminal justice system, all authority, the world).

Prisons are made from concrete and steel, but that hasn't stopped enterprising cons from doing a damn good job of burning down these facilities. They pour cleaning fluid, bleach, and floor wax on their mattresses, causing a strong chemical reaction and fire. With enough heat, the paint on the concrete will start burning, eventually igniting the concrete, too. The roofs, which are usually made of wood and tar, will easily go up in flames. And if, as is more than likely, some prisoners suffer the effects of smoke inhalation, while other cons burn to death in the blaze, it's not like a lot of planning went into staging the event.

Long prison sentences, some with no parole and little opportunity for earning "good time" (reduction in sentence), breed revolt. Somewhere, at this very moment, a "disturbance" is going on in a correctional facility. Few of these come to the attention of the public. Most Departments of Corrections (DOCs) enforce a blackout of news coverage on such incidents because they fear publicity will create contagion—the spreading of rebellion to additional institutions. Typically, the only time the media reports on a prison riot is when convicts take hostages or set an institution on fire, both of which prison rioters are prone to do. Most cellblock uprisings and minor disturbances go unnoticed by reporters outside the walls.

The dramatic growth in the number of institutions has only complicated the problem. In October 1995, during one week, WBET radio in Washington, D.C., reported 38 federal prisons had disturbances. The Prison Activist Center in Berkeley, California, listed at least 15 rioting federal prisons. The national media covered the story of the FBOP riots for one day, then the Feds issued a media prohibition. At FCI Memphis, the riot damage was so extensive that the government had to bulldoze the entire prison. The prison population was temporarily housed in school buses while administrators arranged for transportation to other prisons. One federal prisoner was quoted as saying, "As fast as the BOP builds new prisons, we will burn them down"—a statement sure to be found endearing by taxpayers and law enforcement personnel alike.

In Case of a Riot ...

If you find yourself in the midst of a prison riot, keep your head down and don't get carried away by the excitement. Most lifers know it's wisest to stay in their cells and avoid the frenzy taking place in the corridors. Model your behavior after those lifers, as they have seen it all before and have lived to tell about it.

Remember, no matter what happens, the hacks will eventually retake the institution and press charges against the rioters. If a media crew manages to get inside, stay well out of the cameras' range; the last thing you want is to end up on the nightly news or the front page of a newspaper, as this will probably lead to your indictment, even if you were only a bystander. If you talk to reporters, you'll suddenly be perceived as a ringleader. The best policy is to stay cool, quiet, and out of the limelight.

Passive Resistance

Prisoners have other, more creative, ways to resist authority. Many of these methods are similar to what a child going through the "terrible twos" does when he or she gets stubborn. A con might comply with direct orders, but do it very slowly (sometimes called slow-playing). When an officer tells a group of cons to paint a corridor, which under normal circumstances should take a day, and it ends up taking a week, the cons are slow-playing the job. It's intended to piss the officer off, and it usually works. Alternatively, you can ignore the officer and pretend you're hard of hearing. This frustrates the officer, and he might end up walking away shaking his head.

Another, more involved, action is to file writs, motions, lawsuits, and class action suits. Administrators and officers consider jailhouse lawyers to be some of the most dangerous people in prison because they know how to write up legal motions and get them before a court. At the very least, even if the convicts are denied satisfaction by the legal proceeding, they succeed in embarrassing the prison authorities. It's a form of communicating with the outside about the conditions of confinement, and it scares the prison authorities.

For some real fun, try suing the warden and prison guards personally. That'll put you in solid with them.

Weapons

There are few fistfights in the penitentiary. Most disputes are settled with shanks—homemade weapons made from toothbrushes and razor blades, broken glass and tape, or any metal that can be sharpened and fashioned into either a cutting or stabbing device.

An experienced convict can make a weapon out of nearly anything. A newspaper rolled tight can be used like a knife to thrust at an opponent's vulnerable soft parts. Harden this with toothpaste or plaster and fill it with match heads and a projectile, and you've got yourself a zip gun. Pillowcases filled with soda cans are also handy weapons. Prison yard plants and industrial strength cleaners used on floors and bathrooms can be used as poisons, fire accelerants, or explosives. Strange but true, dental floss is a powerful weapon. It can be used to garrote or strangle a person.

If you carry a weapon, the drawbacks are that you're more likely to use it, someone might be able to use it on you, or you'll get caught with it and be taken to solitary. You'll be cuffed and maybe tuned up (beaten) on your way to the hole, later to be temporarily taken out in handcuffs and shackles for an administrative hearing, told what your punishment is, and then possibly transferred to a higher-security prison.

On the other hand, it's not such a bad idea to have a weapon hidden someplace where you can get your hands on it fast if needed.

Avoiding Fights ✗

Generally, there are a number of rules for avoiding violence in prison.

- **Be very polite, show respect for other convicts, and avoid confrontations.** You never know when some guy is about to go over the edge, and off on you, so it's important to be careful and learn the ways of the penitentiary. When you accidentally brush or bump into another man in the hallway, apologize. Never enter another man's cell or sit on his bed without asking permission. Don't skip in line, in the chow hall or at the commissary, as this may get you killed.

- **Don't run your mouth about your own business or that of other men.** Never talk to guards without another convict present. You don't want to be labeled a snitch or informer. Be careful not to bad rap another convict, as prison is a small world and your words may be repeated.

- **Never show weakness or back down from another convict.** You can stand your ground without the situation becoming a fist fight by using carefully chosen words or demeanor, without antagonizing the other guy. Don't exacerbate things by provoking or antagonizing.

- **Avoid doing business with convict merchants, going into debt, or betting.** The inmate economy is based on cigarettes, alcohol, drugs, sex, and gambling, and it's known for violence. Don't lend anything to or borrow anything from strangers, and only share scarce resources with your clique. Gambling is probably the most dangerous activity in the pen, as convicts will kill gamblers who don't cover their bets.

- **Stay out of television rooms when crowded.** Many federal prisons have television rooms where as many as 100 convicts may be watching a single set. These are dangerous places, especially during sports programming, as many men are compulsive gamblers. If you try to change the channel, they may beat you to death or cut you to ribbons.

■ **Be very careful when using the telephone.** Many prisons have only a few phones available for convicts to call home, and their use is regulated by a sign-up sheet. It's not uncommon for a prisoner to have to wait a week to make a phone call, and only then when his name appears on the time sheet. Convicts are limited to short phone calls, usually collect calls only, or paid for with commissary cards. You are required to give up the phone after only a short time (5–15 minutes). If you linger on past your time and into the next time slot, the man in line behind you will become quite agitated. (And don't forget: All phone calls are monitored by staff and taped. If you complain about the guards, or talk about their crimes and corruption, you may suffer severe consequences.)

There's an old saying in prison, "The only con who wins a fight is the one who walks away, but he better not turn his back." Otherwise, he's liable to get a knife in it. In prison, convicts learn to negotiate or fight, to explain themselves or suffer retribution. He who learns to walk away will be able to renew the conflict at a time and place of his own choosing.

In every cellblock (typically 500 prisoners) there are a couple dozen seething paranoids and violent sociopaths who've armed themselves with deadly weapons. Most likely, they're the guys who will never make it out of the penitentiary alive because, once they're armed, they'll attract the attention of other dangerous paranoids and end up getting killed.

Meanwhile, most convicts somehow manage their daily affairs with carefully crafted social skills. They have learned to get along with most of their fellow convicts and avoid violent prisoners and staff.

Guard Violence

The prison staff do use violence against convicts. They are allowed by law to use force when life and property are in peril. The questions become, how frequently is it used, and is it done in an indiscriminate manner? Most often officers avoid using violence if they can. It creates too much ill will that is remembered for a long time. Instead, they rely on threats. When officers do beat convicts, it's quite often because they have attacked the officer or have instigated work strikes, riots, or escape attempts.

Unlike the deadly violence inflicted by the cons on each other, most guard violence is more subtle. If they've got it in for you, guards may tear up your mail, refuse to turn up the heat, deny you telephone privileges, or toss (search) your cell. In the middle of the night, while you're sleeping, guards may turn the bed over, dumping you on the floor (you shouldn't have been sleeping that soundly in the first place). They're not going to take the time to politely wake you up. The officers might drag you to the floor, handcuff you, and go through all your personal items in search of weapons, drugs, or other contraband items, all of which circulate freely and ubiquitously throughout the joint. If they really hate your guts, the hacks will confiscate pictures of your children, girlfriend or wife, your sheets, clothing, food, and legal papers. Then they may simply leave you lying naked on the floor.

Strip searches, ostensibly used to detect drugs and weapons, are another form of intimidation. If they want, guards can order you to do this five times a day on the cellblock, in the cafeteria, outdoors, or when you come in and out of the visiting room. They can leave you standing naked outside in a snowstorm while you turn blue and get frostbite. Typically, this happens below the gun tower, with machine guns pointed in your direction, all in the freezing weather.

Sometimes, in medium and maximum security prisons, when the guards think you have something stuck up your keister (rectum), as many cons smuggling contraband do, a strip search will include a finger wave. Like a prostate examination, they stick a gloved finger up your rectum, but it's not your doctor gently checking for a colon obstruction or enlarged prostate. It hurts.

Self-Inflicted Violence

Occasionally cons hurt themselves. It's not uncommon for an older prisoner to one day wake up and decide he can't take it anymore. He shakes hands with his buddies in the chow hall and then, during yard time, he walks past the kill zone (the prohibited area next to a wall or fence) and is shot to death by one of the guards in the towers. This is called death by gun tower. Or a prisoner may make a spectacular swan dive from the fifth floor tier down to the cement floor below. That's why, among other reasons, in most joints there is wire mesh extending up from the handrails to the ceilings of the tiers.

Other forms of suicide include hanging, taking a drug overdose, or slitting wrists with broken glass, jagged metal, or plastic. A con committed to killing himself might one night drink a considerable amount of prison hooch (alcohol), or ingest whatever drugs he can get, then place a plastic bag over his head, go to bed, and suffocate in his sleep.

If you plan to attempt suicide, make a neat finish of yourself and don't bungle the job. Otherwise, you'll be locked up in the hole or psychiatric unit. The guards want you to live, if only because if you die, there'll be a big investigation, they'll have a lot of questions to answer, and they'll have a lot of paperwork to complete.

The prison infirmary has few medical personnel and nobody's going to take you out the gate to a civilian hospital—otherwise, there'd be an epidemic of cons faking suicide attempts as a ploy to go to a civilian hospital, to facilitate an escape attempt, or even just to break the monotony. You won't speak to a psychologist or counselor, but more than likely be sent back to the tier when it looks like you've calmed down. If you're in a minimum security facility, they might take you to a hospital. Here an ambulance can make it into and out of the facility relatively quickly, as compared to a penitentiary.

A final form of suicide is the escape attempt. If you try to climb the wall, you will be electrocuted by high voltage lines or cut to ribbons by razor wire. More than likely, you'll die on the wall. If by some freak chance you make it over, odds are you'll be shot down by your pursuers. Escaped convicts are usually wanted dead or alive. Some prisoners suggest that an unofficial policy of the FBOP is to kill the escapee, in order to deter other prisoners from attempting the same desperate flight to freedom. Could be. A successful escapee is a bigger headache for the prison authorities than one shot dead while trying to crash out.

You do time differently depending on the length, sentence, and security level. Some individuals do 20 to 30 years in prison and they don't become killers because that's their nature. They maintain their dignity for decades, like monks. That's how you beat the man.

One of the most important things a prisoner needs to maintain is his or her self-respect. Incarceration is indeed a test of your character and soul.

Gangs ✗

You might assume that when you go to prison you'll be allowed to "do your own time" and, if you stay out of the way of gangs, they'll leave you alone. Unfortunately, your ability to be left to your own devices depends on the prison that you are sent to. Some penitentiaries are literally run by gangs. In those pens, if you don't join one faction or another, you may not be able to defend yourself.

What bothers many convicts, in fact one of their biggest fears, is that once they've decided that they can "do their own time," situations arise where they have to defend themselves, and this inevitably will put them in a position where they'll catch another case and never go home. For example, gang bangers (members) may try to extort cigarettes from you or do a cell invasion in which they simply run into your house and grab your stuff. If you don't retaliate, they'll continue to do it to you. In this case, you may think that it's in your best interest to either join another gang for self-protection or "strap up" (get a shank) and hunt down your perpetrators and stick and cut them.

A number of ethnic and racially based prison gangs exist—i.e., Crips, Bloods, Aryan Brotherhood, Mexican Mafia, Latin Kings, Syndicate. Some, like Colombians (many of whom are affiliated with the drug cartel), are multiracial, which makes trying to identify groups based solely on skin color difficult.

Maximum security prisons have large gang populations. And it goes without saying that gang affiliation will depend on the region of the country you have to do time in. For example, in Illinois and New York you'll find a disproportionate number of Hispanic gangs like the Latin Kings or Vice Lords, or black gangs like the El Rukin or Black Gangster Disciples. In California and Texas you'll find the Mexican Mafia. The longer you do time, you will notice that, much like political parties, gangs have different factions or divisions. In the Mexican organizations, for instance, there are both urban and rural components.

Most of these organizations have been around for decades and have long histories. The public generally thinks that members are teenagers and young adults. Gangs, however, include all different age groups, including junior gangsters, gang warriors (gang bangers), and older gang members. These groups also include wannabes (they want to join), associates (family or friends who are loosely connected to the members), and auxiliaries (lady friends). A few of the senior members may have established legitimate businesses, which employ high-powered accountants and lawyers, and have the resources to buy judges, politicians, and their way out of prison. Some members of the Hell's Angels, for example, are now corporate presidents, or businessmen who own golf courses or car dealerships. Ultimately, gangs are a form of organized crime.

Gang members generally come from large cities. The black gangs of the 1970s, like the Crips and Bloods, first started on the West Coast in Los Angeles. Soon they spread to other cities in California, then made their way across the Midwest to the East Coast, where they set up shop in New York City, Boston, and Philadelphia. Gangs recruit new members in jail and prison and have colonized many state and federal pens. The gang may serve as a surrogate family for members both on the street and in prison, providing those social and emotional needs that only well-adjusted families can provide. In fact, some members call the gang their family.

There are different kinds of gangs. Some exist primarily for economic gain (focusing on business activities like selling drugs, theft, and extortion), while others are formed for mutual self-protection. Some gangs are more violent than others.

Prison gang culture is really an extension of street life into the penitentiary. Traditions learned on the street are simply imported into correctional facilities. For example, rituals of social solidarity, like dancing, singing, and rapping, will make their way into the joint. These forms of informal entertainment originated in ghetto and barrio neighborhoods, where people live in high-density apartment complexes, public housing projects, or small houses, and the kids are forced to play on the streets. Like in the ghetto, action in prison happens in public places, as entertainment is used to display group affiliation and cultural expression. This can lead to some unique activity seen nowhere else, only in prison.

While doing time in Leavenworth, one of the authors of this book remembers the constant clash of culture between urban blacks and rural whites. This was most apparent in the music each group played on their radios or sang. Typically, blacks listened to and sang rhythm and blues, Motown, or rap, while the whites played and crooned country or rock and roll.

One day in the cellblock, a hillbilly country western singer, who liked to belt out Johnny Cash and Merle Haggard songs on the cellblock before lights out, usually to the cheers of "good old boys" and the boos of "the brothers," abruptly changed his tune. Switching from Kentucky Blue Grass, he suddenly broke into Jackie Wilson tunes and then a Motown medley, to the delight of his African-American cellmates. The redneck country boy sounded just like Diana Ross. When he sang Billy Jean, he moon-danced like Michael Jackson up and down the tier.

The "brothers," who couldn't fail to return the compliment, answered with their own rendition of George Jones, Waylon Jennings, and David Alan Coe: "I was drunk the day my mother got out of prison and she got run over by a damned old train." All convicts, regardless of where they're from, enjoy music about Momma, trains, prison, and getting drunk. Besides, music is one way men pass the time, regardless of their gang or skin color. That evening the music even held up the count, as the guards, smiles on their faces, didn't want to interrupt the show.

Membership Has Its Privileges ... and Obligations

Hollywood movies and rap videos make it look like being a gang member is cool. All you have to do to belong is learn the slang and hand signals, wear appropriate clothing (and colors), get the right tattoos, and hang out with the group. Unfortunately, joining a gang carries many obligations and responsibilities you might not enjoy. There is a price to pay for affiliation that may include participating in revenge, retaliation, feuds, even all out gang wars against rival factions that may extend from the "hood" to the penitentiary and last for years. In prison, gang leaders may be locked down in solitary confinement, segregation cells, control units, or supermax prisons.

An important aspect of all gang affiliations is respect. Young men and women who grow up in inner-city neighborhoods want to be respected and not "dissed." And the way respect is typically displayed in the ghetto is by the clothes you wear, the money you spend, and the car you drive. In the joint, gang members can be identified by how they alter their uniforms, share their food and drugs, and walk and dine together in the chow hall and yard.

Gang members often expect to go to prison. When they go to the joint, they try to make themselves comfortable. This means that they want new uniforms that are sharply pressed and a locker full of cigarettes and commissary food. Some want nothing more than to watch NBA basketball every day. In fact, it seems like they would be happy to watch sports programs until the day they die.

In many joints it's not uncommon to find black gangs focus a lot of their attention on sports betting because they find a willing population of prisoners who are more than happy to bet on game after game. Since the standard currency in prison is a carton of cigarettes, it's usually the minimum bet placed. On the other hand, convicted dope dealers, who are used to "living large" and have a lot of money, will bet $10,000 to $20,000 on a game.

Sometimes, however, the betting will lead to complications. Some dude bets a hundred bucks that the Knicks will beat the Celtics. He loses the bet and can't pay up. He tells the gang member that he'll have the money sent in from the outside. If he's lucky, his girlfriend or old lady will mail the money in, and if it's not stolen in the process, it'll be put on his commissary account. Then, because carrying money in prison is considered contraband, he needs to go to the commissary and purchase cigarettes to pay his gambling debt with smokes. Alternatively, if he owes $1,000 dollars, he may have a buddy on the street pay it to the gang on the outside.

The Business of Gangs

Gangs are organized to carry out business, not only on the street but in prison, too. They are responsible for bringing a lot of drugs into the penitentiary. In fact, they pretty much have a monopoly on this line of work in most correctional facilities. Why? Plain and simple: There is considerable profit to be made. Prices for drugs in prison are highly inflated from their street value. Gang members distribute dope, especially cocaine and heroin (because they're easy to conceal), on the cellblocks on a regular basis.

Gangs use many methods to get drugs into prisons. They have 24 hours a day to figure out how to beat the security systems and protocols. The most common method is to have visitors bring drugs into the visiting room and pass it mouth to mouth. What to the guards looks like a long, passionate kiss is actually the transfer of a small balloon or a condom containing dope, which the prisoner swallows and then fishes out of his stool later that day. Gang members on the outside also often simply throw the drugs, inside a tennis ball, over the wall or fence or use slingshots to propel the drugs. Small planes also occasionally fly over prisons at night and drop the drugs into the yard.

Gang members may also recruit or force correctional officers to bring drugs into prison. They may compromise them by threatening to turn them in for illegal behavior they observe or hear about. Another way to "get the goods on them" is to catch hacks doing drugs themselves or having sex with a prisoner. In some correctional facilities, gay prison guards may actually fall in love with a male prisoner.

Alternatively, a convict may successfully threaten the officer's family by finding out where they live. All they need is a buddy (or fellow gang member) to snap a photo of the guard's spouse, children, or house, and then show it to the officer.

Some correctional officers, because they are paid so little, smuggle contraband into the joint because they see it as an opportunity to buy a new pickup truck or retire early. In fact, many convicts will tell you that the majority of drugs are brought in by guards who are in business for themselves. For example, the correctional officer may only make $20,000 a year, but he has a friend or a brother-in-law who occasionally sells drugs, and he can make $100,000 a year through this connection.

Finally, a sophisticated gang like the Bloods or Crips may actually get new gang members or wannabes (who don't have a criminal record) to apply for a job with the state Department of Corrections. Some jurisdictions are so desperate for employees and have such minimal requirements that they will employ anyone who doesn't have a felony conviction. If hired, the person then acts as the go-between to smuggle drugs and other forms of contraband into the prison.

Hangin' with Your Gang

When black and Hispanic gangs dominate a prison, the whites will group together for mutual protection. For example, in the California joints, where gang conflicts are common, some of the Blue Birds and Hell's Angels of San Quentin (motorcycle gangs) eventually became the white supremacist Aryan Brotherhood. If you're in a gang, you basically "hang together." This means eating as a group in the cafeteria, walking the yard together, pumping iron (lifting weights), and sticking close to each other at work assignments or in housing units.

If you're a gang member on the outside, when you go to prison those inside your new facility might already have heard about you. Your "rep" (your reputation) will have preceded you. And you may already know people who were from different gangs or with whom you had business dealings on the street.

Once inside, your gang friends might tell you who you should see or check out if you get transferred. They may say, "If you ever get to such-and-such prison, you should connect with a group of people that no one will mess with." One of the authors, for example, played a lot of bocci (an Italian form of bowling) with Mafia members; when others noticed this fraternizing, they thought he was hooked up to Don Corleone.

In some prisons you absolutely need to affiliate with a group that will protect you. The loners, the people without social skills or friends, are vulnerable to being physically attacked or preyed upon.

Despite the violence and gangs, life in the penitentiary goes on. One day leads to the next, and to the next, and to the next ...

Chapter 10

Brother, Can You Spare Some Time: A Day in the Life of Joe Convict

Having been assaulted with the reality of prisons, perhaps you would benefit from spending a day as Joe Convict. We trace your daily routine from the time you (and 500 other convicts) are let out of your cage (cell) in the morning through the rest of your day. We'll look at some of the obstacles you need to overcome just to get a crumb of food to sustain yourself, to avoid losing your life, and to maintain some semblance of sanity at the same time.

6 A.M. Rise and Shine

You, Joe Convict, live in cell 562 on the fifth tier of cellblock A. The population of this maximum security institution is 2,000 men living in four cell blocks: A, B, C, and D. It's Monday morning. You don't need an alarm clock in prison, not when the lights come on at 6 A.M. and you wake to the noise of 500 or more men urinating, flushing toilets, coughing, stirring, rustling about their cells for their clothing, and getting dressed.

8 A.M. Count

You're still in your bunk when the guards start yelling, "Count/la cuenta!" All the metal cell doors automatically come open at once with a loud bang. Even a sound sleeper will be jarred awake because of the noise. You're wearing your uniform, which you slept in. You don't sleep in pajamas. You've been issued two sheets, a thin army blanket, and a foam pillow, so you need all the warmth you can get.

It's a winter morning in the penitentiary, with the temperature outside reading five below zero. Ice has formed on the windows and on some of the walls and floors. You stand on the frigid cement just outside your open cage for count. This will be the first of six counts that day, each four hours apart. Convicts use the count as a means to tell the time of day. Guards use the count as a means to see if any inmates are out of place, dead, or missing altogether.

Two guards are walking the tiers. They start on the first and walk past each cell, counting every man. When they get to the end of the tier, they check the number, then proceed to the second range (tier or floor). It'll take them roughly 20 minutes to get up to the fifth floor. Meanwhile, your neighbor is standing there freezing because on that day he was slow in getting dressed. On most days cons don't say anything to the prisoners in the adjoining cells—it's against prison rules to talk during count. If you don't step out of your cell, the guards can throw you in the hole. Move too slowly when the automatic doors close, and they can take your head off—they're not safety-fitted like elevator doors. If you're sick, you still must come out of your cell or risk being cuffed and dragged to the hole.

The guards walk past you, counting as they go, and then descend the staircase back to the first floor. From down below you hear the hacks yell "count clear." Now you're free to resume dressing and getting ready for breakfast. You don't have to worry about taking a shower that day, as you took one a couple of days ago.

Unlike some institutions that have showers in each individual cell, at this joint they're on the end of the tier, and some days it's too impractical to use them because of overcrowding. Showers are open 16 hours a day, in a communal type arrangement, like you would find in a men's locker room. Guards don't supervise men in this area (they don't want to get wet or they can't see anything because of the steam), which is why assaults, rapes, and killings happen here.

There are certain people you just don't want to shower next to. Some days, after looking forward all week to a shower, you see some dude in the room who you know is bad news, so you make a 180-degree turn and return to your cell. Or on a day like today, because of freezing weather, the pipes might have frozen solid or burst. Or there are 100 men taking a shower. It's like being at the baseball game or the unemployment office: There is always a long line.

Maybe you'll take your shower later in the day. Who cares, as long as you don't stink too badly? You take care of most of your personal hygiene in your cell. The toilet is a one-piece stainless steel unit, and there is hot water available from a small sink, assuming it works. You wash your body with a wet towel.

You put on your black convict work boots with the reinforced metal toes (potentially a lethal weapon in combat) and your military field jacket (army fatigue coat). You step out of your cell again, and see that men everywhere are stirring, smoking cigarettes, and bullshitting. You peer over the railing and hear the guards talking on their walkie-talkies as they communicate with guards on other cellblocks to check the count. If a con happens to be found dead in his cell, even in another housing unit, they lock everybody up in their cages. The police (FBI or state troopers) come in to do an investigation, and this can last two or three days. Meals will be brought to the cells. These will be box lunches consisting of cheese sandwiches, apples, and a carton of milk.

Today, as always, you hope that no one died in his sleep. If your family was coming to visit you or you promised them that you'd call, you'd be screwed. Surrounding motels would be filled with families who came to see their sons, husbands, and brothers, but can't until the lockdown is lifted.

Controlled Movement

The guards finally get the word that the count is clear for the entire institution. If you want to go to breakfast, you line up single file and walk down the stairs to the cell-house security gate, where an officer counts each man as he walks out into the main corridor. If you don't want breakfast, you can stay in your housing unit.

This is a controlled movement penitentiary, where officers are posted throughout the institution. As you proceed down the corridor, you are monitored by video cameras in the ceiling and guards standing with their backs to the wall on either side of you. Your cell-house of 500 men then stands in front of another steel door monitored by officers in a steel and glass booth, who hit the button and count you as you walk through that door. Finally, you arrive at the dining hall. The cafeteria, with its plastic tables and seats, looks like a giant McDonald's without the Happy Meals. You politely take your place in line with the rest of the prison population that was willing to take a risk on the food that day.

At 9 A.M., breakfast is over, and there's another controlled movement. In the penitentiary you move on the hour, like high school. Depending on the prison, a bell, whistle, or horn signals movement changes; some prisons don't use any auditory signal at all. In either case, you are expected to know and anticipate the controlled movement. It's part of the routine to be released to go to your workstation, which might be mopping floors, working in the kitchen, clerking in education, medical, or administration departments, or laboring in one of a number of factories.

You have 10 minutes to get to your factory job, where you'll again be counted. From 9:10 A.M. till noon you work making mailbags, license plates, office furniture, products for a military contractor, or whatever it is that the factory produces.

In some penitentiaries, armed guards walk the catwalks above you. Still, in most plants, you don't work very hard. You sit around talking to your buddies. In a factory of 400 guys, only about 50 will be really working—the rest of the men while away the time pretending to work. The prison foreman, who's a guard, can do very little to motivate the workers. He can fire them, whereupon they will be replaced by guys who are much the same. Would you work hard for 10 cents an hour?

Noon Count

At noon there will be another count and, when it clears, there will be another controlled movement, during which you may go to the dining hall for lunch. New prisoners worry that if they're at the wrong place at the wrong time, they'll be thrown in the hole. Old prisoners, on the other hand, are so accustomed to the count that they can almost feel it in their bones.

If it's a nice day, you might just wander about the yard and eat locker food out of your pocket. It depends on the institution and how you feel at the time. Today, you know the cafeteria is going to be serving macaroni and cheese. The last time they served it, it was passable; plus you're getting tired of eating out of your locker, and you're low on commissary food, so you decide to try the chow hall. You make your way to the cafeteria, where you take your place in line. Today, because you're not alone in thinking that the meal might be a safe bet, you discover about 1,500 other convicts acting on the same idea.

You get in line, pick up a plastic tray and plastic spoon, and proceed to fill a plastic cup with Kool-Aid. You slide your tray over to where the hot food is being served, where you have a choice of mashed potatoes, green beans, and what you came for, the mac and cheese. You skip the salad bar because all the lettuce is brown and cockroach-infested. Last Monday morning, some local dignitaries were given a tour of the facilities, and the salad actually was green, but now it's not.

You take a seat at a table with your factory mates. There'll be some conversation. Generally, the dining hall will be divided based on skin color, with whites sitting with whites, blacks with blacks, and Hispanics with Hispanics. The guards eat in a separate dining hall or out of bag lunches. If by chance you land in an institution where the guards eat with the prisoners, the food will be better. No such luck at this joint. When you finish your lunch, you may go back up and get some cookies, which were probably baked that same day and are the only thing in the kitchen that's really fresh. You stick them in a plastic bag in your pocket.

Unfortunately, as you run the gauntlet of officers standing a few feet apart at the dining room exit, your luck runs out. As you're walking out, one of the guards pulls you aside and orders you to stand still while he searches your clothing. You're busted, as the guard discovers the "stolen" food and yells at you for being a thief, threatening you with a trip to the hole.

You keep your cool, mumbling some line about how sorry you are, and the officer allows you return to the factory without getting a shot. It's a routine that's played out at every meal between the cons and the guards lined up at the door. The cons have to walk past the guards, who eyeball each prisoner, attempting to discern who's stealing food. This is actually a good test of how good a shoplifter you are. Many of the guards don't even care about the stolen food, but they follow orders from their bosses.

In terms of hygiene, it makes sense. Correctional facilities have big problems with cockroaches and rats that are attracted to food crumbs. Still, the institution doesn't hesitate to sell you all the commissary food you can buy, knowing that guys eat in their cells. Maybe they think the rats prefer the cafeteria food to the commissary food, or maybe it's that every piece of food taken out of the cafeteria is just that much less sold out of the commissary.

The administrative logic is easy to understand: They want to spend as little money as possible on the bare necessities (i.e., food, clothing, heat, medical services). They really don't give a damn whether you eat the cafeteria food or not. In terms of the institution as a whole, they make money with the commissary, and not with the cafeteria.

4 P.M. Count

After lunch, at 1 P.M., there's another controlled movement. You go back to the factory where you work until 5 P.M. An hour before quitting time, there's another count, the "major count." While the guards may have fudged the numbers on earlier counts, letting everyone move even if they didn't get an accurate count, if they don't get it right this time, no one budges. You, along with your buddies, remain at your workstation. You can't even leave your workbench to, say, go to the bathroom. Nobody goes anywhere until this one clears. The cons are happy today, because on Friday the major count took two hours to clear and today's was only 30 minutes.

At 5 P.M., there's another controlled movement. You leave the factory to go to the yard for an hour. In the yard, rain or shine, no matter if it's freezing cold—as it is today—you'll stand there talking to your friends, trading prison gossip, rumors, and the latest scuttle-butt. Your clique tells you who's in solitary, whose cell got tossed, maybe about how an old con died from lack of medical attention. More generally, they tell stories about their lives, who they once were, and what they want to do when they get out. Some guys might even wax philosophical, con-style, but mostly they stand and look at the tall walls and think about home.

At 6 P.M., you decide to skip dinner to return to the cellblock. Salisbury steak (or so they call it) is on the menu, and the last time you ate it, you threw up. You don't want to chance it again. Besides, because you work in the factory, you made commissary that month, and you've still got some instant soups in your locker—if there's enough hot water running through the pipes in your cell, you'll heat up some of that soup. Otherwise, it's down to the communal bathroom to find hot water. You drink the soup because you don't have any utensils. Although it'd be convenient to steal one of those plastic cafeteria spoons, if you're caught with one, the guards will accuse you of possessing contraband, and then you're off on a trip to the hole.

That evening, you lay down on your bunk in the cell, reading the famous Russian author Solzhenitsyn's book on his 10-year imprisonment in the Soviet gulag. There's a count at 8 P.M., and two more scheduled for later that night—one at midnight and one at 4 A.M.—but you won't have to stand for any of these. You'll be counted while you're sleeping, by officers who shine flashlights as they walk from cell to cell. While you sleep, you're required to "show skin," which means that you must expose a foot, leg, hand, or face to the guards' flashlights as they do their count.

Lights Out

At 10 P.M., it's lights out. As night descends on the cellblock, the sounds can be eerie, even haunting. Above the constant drone of men snoring and turning in their sleep, strange noises rise from the steel tiers. One man is praying to Jesus, another to Allah, and a third to God knows whom. Other men weep or moan, as they are visited by nightmares that will not fade. The war veterans bounce off the steel walls, as they relive the horror of combat alone in their cells with no one to ease their fears. The most frightening sounds are those of men crying for their children.

Strange thoughts occupy your mind late at night in the penitentiary. Tonight, you wake up in a sweat, confused as to whether your dream was any better than the living nightmare of this federal pen. At least you're alive, which is more than you can say for some of the cons you've known over the years, who've been shot by guards and shanked by cons.

After being in prison for a long time, some cons act like robots. Prisoners don't need to think for themselves. The routine moves you from place to place. You can almost always predict what's next. If a television is available, some cons will sit in front of it all day long. They know all the soap operas, what time they're on, and who the stars are. In some places during the weekend, to break up the monotony, there's a movie.

There it is, one day in the life of a convict. Your life. If you're smart, you'll avoid thinking about all the other, near-identical days of confinement stretching ahead of you, the weeks, months, and years. That way lies madness.

Chapter 11

We Ain't No Debutantes: Women Behind Bars

Over the past two centuries, conditions have improved for women in prisons. During the nineteenth century, in England and the United States, most women prisoners weren't separated from the men, which inevitably led to physical and sexual abuse. Even when they were confined in a separate wing of a prison for men, they were vulnerable to abuse by male administrators, guards, and prisoners.

A number of women reformers championed the cause of female prisoners, and by the twentieth century many states and the federal government established prisons solely for women and increasingly staffed those prisons with women. Partially because of the war on drugs, partly because of stiffer mandatory sentencing guidelines, and perhaps also because women have been accepted, if not as equals, than at least as partners or associates in crime, a considerable number of females have entered the prison system in the past two decades. Since 1983, it's estimated that the number of women in prison has grown by 344 percent, as compared to 207 percent for men. Today we have close to 150,000 females serving time in jails and prisons. Women now make up nearly 10 percent of the U.S. prison population.

Women's Joints

Nearly every state has at least one prison for women. Some of the more sparsely populated states, which may have a total of 50 women convicts, end up shipping their prisoners to a neighboring state or housing them in separate wings of county jails.

There are no maximum security or supermax federal prisons for connets, as women prisoners are commonly referred to, in the United States. The highest-security correctional facility for women resembles a medium security prison for men. For example, the Federal Prison Camp in Lexington Women's Facility houses 400 connets, including some serving life sentences, yet has no fence or gun towers. Even though it would be easy enough to walk away from these facilities, escapes from women's prisons are rare events.

If there were more women in correctional custody and if more connets attempted to escape, you can be sure that state and federal planners would install additional security features. Instead, women in prison for murder are typically behind bars for killing their boyfriends, spouses, or children. Correctional systems don't erect sophisticated security because they don't expect these women to escape and kill strangers.

Why Women Do Time

Generally, women are sentenced to jail or prison for frequent convictions of petty crimes. For example, a woman is convicted of shoplifting 10 separate times, then comes in front of a judge who's exasperated and "throws the book at her," sentencing her to three years at the state prison for women. Not only do women go to jail and prison for multiple convictions for shoplifting, but they also arrive at the gates for possession of drugs, small-scale drug dealing, embezzlement, credit card fraud, and writing bad checks.

If arrests are any indication of why women are being incarcerated, we can look at FBI statistics. In 1997, out of a total of 2,000,818 women arrested, they were primarily picked up for crime of poverty (358,210 women), larceny or theft (314,468), and violent crime (71,194). Of the crimes for which women are serving time, approximately 32 percent are violent, 33 percent are connected to drugs and/or alcohol, 25 percent are property-related, 4 percent are victimless, and 6 percent fall into other categories.

Women are less likely to have a history of committing violent crimes than male cons. When they kill, it's usually their fathers, husbands, boyfriends, or children; women rarely kill people they don't know. Women usually kill their husbands while they are asleep, after the men have abused them. And despite more women charged with serious drug felonies, they are typically accessories rather than the principal actors.

A typical connet is single, in her late twenties, and was struggling to survive poor economic circumstances before she was incarcerated. She has never finished high school, and has a couple of children. She may have dropped out of school somewhere around the ninth grade because she got pregnant and had no one to take care of her child. She never acquired a formal education that would allow her anything more than a low-paying job like hotel maid or kitchen staff. She periodically, if not totally, depends on public assistance. She has a history of being physically abused by men, the first time when she was a teenager. She uses alcohol and/or drugs, and has been arrested many times.

Women's prisons are filled with illiterate females, many of them minorities, who've struggled at a succession of low-paying jobs in order to make ends meet.

How Women Do Time

Women in prison are less violent and more supportive of their sister cons than men. Often, groups of connets will form a pseudo family, with older women assuming the role of father and mother and younger convicts as children. These "families" will walk the yard together, eat at the same table, and share their meager resources, much like any other struggling family. It provides some women with something that they've always longed for: the semblance of a stable family situation. This may be the only chance in their life to live out these idealized roles.

Jobs in the Joint

In the joint, women perform a lot of the same jobs men do, including cooking, mopping floors, routine maintenance, and groundskeeping. There may even be a small factory where the women work for commissary money. If there is some sort of vocational training, it tends to be for sex-role based positions, such as cosmetologist, seamstress, and domestic servant.

A lot of women's prisons train the cons in telemarketing. In Wisconsin, the entire state lottery system is run out of a state prison for women. Also, many credit card, airline, and mail-order catalogue companies operate phone sales out of these institutions. In order to prevent the convicts from using your credit card to buy stuff for themselves, relatives, or friends, guards frisk the prisoners before they leave their work site. Of course, that presupposes that convicts won't somehow write down or memorize the information for later use, a perhaps over-optimistic assumption. Most of the programs where female cons process credit card numbers are in minimum security prisons, where administrators believe that the prisoners are less likely to engage in these types of scams.

Like men's prisons, women's facilities have minimal educational services and few or no counseling and parenting skills workshops.

Connet Violence

Connets are less violent than their male counterparts, have fewer formal complaint reports against them, and are more supportive of their sister cons.

Still, women may push, slap, punch, and kick each other. They generally don't stab or kill one another, and their fights don't have high mortality rates. Female cons rarely carry shanks. However, a 300-pound female convict is capable of inflicting serious physical damage on an opponent.

Staff Violence

Male staff in women's prisons have a history of sexually abusing female prisoners. In most states, any sexual relations between prison staff and prisoners is considered by law to be sexual assault or rape. In the joint, there's no such thing as consensual sex between the keepers and the kept. Hundreds of prison guards have been fired and/or indicted on sexual assault charges.

Some state prison systems, like Georgia, have implemented tough "no touch, no contact" policies. Men are not allowed to supervise women convicts. If a male enters the unit, the announcement "man or male on range" can be heard. At some federal prisons for women, administrators have even installed hotlines where female prisoners can make complaints if they've been sexually abused. Sometimes this is a public relations exercise designed to garner support from the wider public to show them that something is being done about this problem. Still, today there are a number of states that haven't outlawed staff-inmate sex.

Mothers in Prison

Many women prisoners are mothers, who may feel that their children have been abandoned to the makeshift care of relatives or social service agencies when they were imprisoned. Although both men and women often worry about their children while they are incarcerated, when fathers are in prison, their wives or girlfriends are probably taking care of their children. In contrast, when mothers serve time, their children are more likely to be relegated to a relative or social service agency, placed in a foster home, or put up for adoption.

Let's say a woman is a heroin addict with a long prison record. In addition to the criminal charge that brought her into the prison system, she may also be accused of child abuse or neglect, and her children are taken from her. If she's lucky and gets along with her relatives, perhaps they will take in the children. To grant custody, however, a judgment has to take place to see if the relative is a suitable parent.

Some women prisoners were great mothers before they went to prison, but because of their crimes, their kids have been legally removed from their custody. Incarcerated mothers must worry about worst-case scenarios, for example: Her spouse divorces her in prison, remarries and moves to another state with the children, and she never sees the kids again. Connets who've had their children taken away often are wracked with remorse about their criminal behavior.

Giving Birth Behind Bars

Many women enter prison pregnant and give birth to their children while serving time. According to U.S. government statistics, as many as 6 percent of the women entering state and federal prisons are pregnant. There are no reliable statistics on the number of pregnancies that result in termination, miscarriage, or are carried to term. While we know that at least a couple thousand children are born to convict mothers, we don't really know what happens to them. Worse, women prisoners have been raped by guards while incarcerated, and were forced to give birth to the offspring.

When a prisoner goes through childbirth, she's handcuffed and transferred to a civilian hospital. The cuffs aren't taken off while she goes through labor and during delivery. With luck, the baby will be taken in by a relative. More likely, the baby is turned over to foster care or put up for adoption.

A very small number of prisons may allow a mother to care for her newborn for a short time in the prison. For example, in most large jails, like Rikers in New York City, they have a neonatal center. But this usually only happens if the female prisoners will be getting out shortly, perhaps within a few weeks, and so neither they nor their babies will be a burden for the system.

Some people mistakenly believe that a pregnant woman can be absolved from going to prison. Contrary to what may have taken place during an earlier time in our nation's history, when it comes to sentencing a woman, the courts no longer care if she's pregnant. Carrying a child doesn't provide any protection from being sent to prison or supply an excuse for immediate release.

Sex

There seems to be more homosexual activity in women's prisons than in men's prisons. While there are no reliable estimates, women in prison do openly show more affection to one another, which may or may not indicate homosexual love. It may be that women are more flexible in their sexual orientation then men.

When Connets Come Home

After release from prison, the first thing women prisoners who have kids do is look for their children. Like the men (see next chapter), they leave the prison with little money, no place of their own to live, and no job. They usually stay with relatives or complete their sentences in halfway houses. Some of these facilities, which are often located in ghetto neighborhoods, are pretty depressing. Pass by one on a hot summer day, and you'll see connets congregating on the front steps, while cars filled with leering men cruise by looking for new girlfriends or recruits to work in their businesses. Some of the women will remain in the house, frightened of the pimps and drug dealers, but others may actively participate in this ritual and start checking out the guys. Most of these women will return to a life of dependency, including social service agency handouts or the games of the street.

Part 4

Beyond the Walls

Chapter 12

Happy Days Are Here Again: Getting Out

In some states, a life sentence really means until the day you die. Unless you've been given such a sanction, or condemned to death, sooner or later you're going to leave the joint. Most prisoners dream about the day that they'll return to the community, to be reunited with loved ones, free to eat a meal in a restaurant, walk down the street, or drive a Lincoln Continental convertible down a coastal highway with the wind blowing in their face.

But the road to freedom is not a smooth one. It's important to be realistic and realize that the cards are statistically stacked against you. Over 50 percent of men released from prison will be returned to the joint in the first year. Fifty percent—in one year!

So be sure to think through your plans and examine every detail. Remember, you're probably not really free; instead, you're on parole or in community supervision and have years to do "on paper." One misstep, and you'll end up back in the slammer.

Re-entry

As a rocket that's been orbiting out in space re-enters the earth's atmosphere, it generates a tremendous amount of heat. As you get out of prison and return home to the community, you may feel just like that spacecraft. Make sure that you land safely and avoid burning up in mid-air. For many prisoners, the transition is complicated by such "heat factors" as the parole system, getting a suitable job, finding a place to live, and rekindling relationships with your spouse—or opening up lines of communication with your ex-wife—and getting on the same level as the kids.

Even before you are released, you may make extensive preparations, including going before the parole board, meeting with your case manager, writing a parole plan, going through a prerelease program, and psychologically getting your mind right and ready for the day you leave.

Stories of Disorientation

When they come out of prison, most men are disoriented and have to make major psychological readjustments. To suggest that these convicts are a little shaky on their feet when they're released is an understatement. Most have "get out of prison" stories about how they'd forgotten how to time the flow of pedestrians on the sidewalk or traffic on the street and experienced great difficulty simply walking around town. Others who've spent a considerable period of time behind bars become disoriented with new technologies, like those found in late model cars. Even the inability to find the high-beam dimmer switch may trigger a crisis of confidence.

One prisoner we know, who served nearly 50 years in maximum security, went to a supermarket. The last time he'd been shopping for groceries had been the 1930s. He became so surprised by the store's automatic doors and electronic checkout counters that he drew the attention of the store manager, who then called the police. After the cops showed up, the man was arrested for disorderly conduct. After getting out of jail, he reported to his parole officer, stabbed him in the neck, and then was transported back to prison.

Depending on the length of time spent in the joint, prisoners may have little memory of what passes for everyday social conventions in the outside world. They may be shy or withdrawn and unable to carry on a casual conversation. The longer people are inside, the more acclimated they will be to the routine of prison time, and the more difficulty they may have readjusting to daily events on the street.

Convicts released from the penitentiary go through a euphoric stage, when they rediscover free time, open space, and new possibilities. This initial infatuation with freedom is frequently short-lived.

Joint Mentality

Convicts suffer from a kind of joint mentality. They walk, talk, and keep time like prisoners. Men and women who've served years of prison time have their own cultural traditions and reality. Their futures are limited by their criminal histories. Ex-convicts experience stigma and discrimination, high rates of recidivism, limited opportunities, an altered perception of time, and above all, the loss of the ability to plan a coherent future.

Many of those who live outside prison walls take their freedom for granted, a luxury denied to the ex-con, whose joint mentality causes him to live day to day, like he did in confinement, without anticipating or planning future events.

Mandatory Release and Parole

Once you've completed your entire determinant sentence, you're given mandatory release (MR). When you're given MR, it means that your entire sentence is done and you're not obligated to go to a halfway house or report to a parole officer.

Most persons released from state prisons have earned "good time" and get out before they've served their entire sentence, for example 25, 33, 50, or 75 percent of their time. They are required to do the rest of their time on parole, which means being on a short leash and subject to return to prison for minor violations of technical rules, with no right to due process. Not all states have parole.

Federal prisoners all have two sentences. The first is the time they will do behind bars; they have to complete 85 percent of this sentence before release to the street. The second sentence is called community supervision. It isn't the same as parole, because it's not based on good time.

Typically, 50 percent of parolees will be returned to the can within one year, and 70 percent within three years. Most of these parole failures will be for technical violations of parole rules: failure to report, testing positive for illegal drugs, not paying court costs or restitution, or being unemployed. Only a small number will actually be returned to prison on a new conviction. Generally, the longer a person is in prison, and the fewer family members that remain in touch with him, the more likely it will be that he fails parole.

The rules of parole include living in a specified city, county, or state, reporting on a regular basis to a parole officer, filing monthly reports with the parole office, not acting as a police informer, not associating with persons who have a criminal record, not possessing firearms, not drinking alcoholic beverages, keeping steady employment, and making a diligent effort to satisfy any court order for fines, restitution, or child support. Of course, if the prisoner finds the requirements too onerous, he or she may decline parole and finish serving out the rest of the sentence in prison.

Prisoners have lived in a society built of cement and steel and share a worldview predicated on their experience of incarceration. They are tentative and insecure, for they know that society isn't as free as they may once have believed. Typically, the sufferings of those they've victimized on the road to the penitentiary is of less concern to them than the injustices they feel they've been subjected to by the criminal justice system, cops, judges, hacks, and ex-spouses ...

Pre-release Programs

Numerous pre-release programs exist, including furloughs, work release, educational release, and halfway houses. A furlough is when you temporarily get out of prison for 24 hours, three days, or maybe even a week for some special purpose. Educational release is when a prisoner serving time in a low-security institution leaves the facility every day to attend community college or university. Work release refers to a program in which a convict is allowed to leave a minimum security camp or halfway house every day to work in the community. A halfway house is a generic term for any facility operated by a government or non-profit agency where prisoners live for a few months upon leaving prison. All these programs have their situational advantages and disadvantages.

Furlough

Some prison systems authorize minimum security prisoners who are within one year of release to go home for a few days to see family and attempt to arrange future housing and employment. Convicts may also qualify for furloughs to get critical medical attention, to attend the burial of a family member, or to participate in religious instruction or services. Some minimum security facilities may allow for unescorted furlough transfers from one camp to another. In general, the prisoner must return to prison at the end of the furlough.

Most prison systems no longer offer furloughs, and even when they do, it's difficult to qualify for them. Too bad, because furloughs are a great way for convicts to readjust to the outside. It affords them an opportunity to test out their plans for release, including finding an appropriate place to live and a job.

Educational Release

A few prisons may still allow model prisoners to leave minimum security institutions to attend community college or university. This presupposes that the prisoner can afford to pay for tuition and books and can complete college level or university courses, that the correctional facility is relatively close to an educational institution, and that the prison will provide transportation. It's not like you go to the parking lot, climb in your car, and drive yourself to campus.

These special programs are very limited, but when they exist, they provide a few seriously motivated prisoners the opportunity to pursue higher education. Of course, if the prisoner enrolls in classes, pays tuition, and then gets a shot, he or she is thereby prevented from attending any further classes.

Work Release

A work release center is a community halfway house with controlled movement, where they release men or women to work for paid employment. They let you out eight hours a day, and then you have to return. At work release facilities, the doors and windows are locked and the prisoners are counted. These community prisoners can be charged with disciplinary violations and be returned to prison for refusing the first available menial job or failing to return promptly to the work release center. Predictably, there is a high rate of failure in these programs.

When people on the outside work, it's usually to support a family, to save for a goal, or because it's a job they love. Often, work release prisoners don't have any of these reasons for getting up in the morning and going off to a job that's usually eight hours of drudgery. What little money they do make is controlled by correctional staff, with much of the pay deducted to pay court-ordered fines and restitution, a little set aside for spending, and the rest put in savings for when they are released. It's easy to see why many work release prisoners are ambivalent about working and why so many of them are sent back to prison within the first three months.

Halfway Houses

Many states have both "halfway in" and "halfway out" residential correctional facilities. The former refers to a community residence, usually reserved for juveniles or young adults, where as part of their probation they may serve a short sentence instead of going to prison. The latter is the traditional facility where men or women stay upon release from prison.

Despite their name, halfway houses are not homes; they are correctional institutions with guards and controlled movement. Many prisoners complain that these facilities have a high failure rate, set unrealistic expectations for residents, and charge exorbitant fees for room and board. Some penitentiary convicts will actually refuse assignment to halfway houses, as they don't trust the correctional authorities to give them an even break. When you get to a halfway house, you're told to get a job. The check is mailed to the halfway house, where the officers cash the check and deduct money for court cost restitution, child support, unpaid taxes, and your keep.

In some cities where there is high employment and low-level jobs are difficult to fill, halfway houses thrive. Although cons can't work cash registers, they can take out trash and flip burgers at minimum skill jobs, with minimum pay to match. Although you may want to use your paycheck to buy some fancier clothes that may help you get a better job, the halfway house typically ends up taking it all. In some jurisdictions, you may even be required to pay for court-ordered substance abuse or anger management courses. After a few weeks you realize that the personnel are taking all your money. Cons see this arrangement as sort of like indentured servitude, a feudal arrangement, sharecropping, or what they call "work release slavery." Of course, taxpayers and crime victims may see it somewhat differently.

Electronic Jackets

Community prisoners are often tracked by computer information systems and returned to prison when they fail to comply with court orders to pay restitution, fines, or child support; don't take their prescribed medication; or don't do community service they are sentenced to perform. Surveillance protocols now include reporting by employers, teachers, and medical personnel. If the community prisoner doesn't show up for work, school, or medical treatment, he or she is often returned to jail or prison. The community correctional penal machinery, once intended to support and assist cons' re-entry into society, is now used to supervise and monitor a growing number of men and women released from prison.

The U.S. Department of Justice, police departments, and courts keep criminal history records on every con and ex-con, and they sell this information to the public. These are used to do background checks for employment, licensing, and security systems that provide information about both arrests and convictions to public and private sector employers.

A considerable amount of what most people automatically assume is private information is available to law enforcement agencies and private businesses throughout the United States. These records, including pre-sentence investigations (PSI) and inmate central files, can be purchased through government offices for a modest fee.

Prisoners and others argue that making criminal records available to the public perpetuates officially sanctioned stigmatization. They fear this information will be used as punishment—additional baggage ex-cons have to carry with them—once they've already served their time. Others claim that the dissemination of matters of public record is simply exercising constitutionally guaranteed First Amendment rights of freedom of speech. No matter which side of the debate you're on, the fact remains that the availability of such information makes the ex-con's already difficult task of getting a job, renting an apartment, or getting a loan even tougher.

The Day You're Released

On the day you get out, you may be lucky enough to have your spouse or other relatives pick you up outside the gate. More often than not, you'll be released from prison wearing your prison uniform, carrying a cardboard box, with five dollars gate money in your pocket. A Greyhound bus picks you up, you hop on it, and you go to the nearest city where you plan to reside. For the next few weeks things will be a little shaky.

Some things to be aware of in the immediate aftermath of your release are the food you eat, finding a job, reestablishing connections with your children, and finding a place to live.

Food on the Outside

The first day you get out of prison, you might want to go to a fancy restaurant and eat a big meal. Be careful. You've been eating simple fare for many months or years. You're not ready for exotic spices and sauces. Your system is not ready for Szechuan Chinese, Thai, or Cajun cooking. You don't want to get sick your first day home, so take it easy. Use moderation.

The food you ate in prison will be the last thing you'll ever want again. You'll never be able to look at a can of tuna, instant soup, or cheap cuts of pork the same way again. Better stick to meat and potatoes.

Looking for Love

Naturally you'll want to get some of your emotional or sexual needs met. Maybe your spouse has even remained faithful to you. If not, you may be tempted to go to the nearest bar to pick up one of those women you've been dreaming about during your long stint inside.

Don't do it. Your release papers state that you can't go to an establishment that serves liquor. Also, keep in mind that when you're looking to have your sexual needs filled, most any woman will look good to you. But you're probably a little older than when you went into prison, and more than likely the lady you'll hook up with will have her own baggage, such as kids, an ex or two, and lots of bills. Too often, guys who immediately start living with a new woman who has a lot of obligations can't help them enough, but they want to play hero, so they go back into some illegal activity to earn money. The next thing you know, they're back in the joint while she's found another live-in lover.

You can't make up for your years inside in one night, so don't even try.

If your spouse, woman, significant other, or whatever, is willing to let you back into her life, don't start asking her a lot of questions about who she was dating, shacking up with, or sleeping with. If you find some strange man's clothing in her closet or shoes under the bed that aren't yours, don't get upset, because it's water under the bridge.

If your wife divorced you while you were in prison, you'll be lucky if she still accepts your phone calls. You won't be welcome on her doorstep. Maybe you can charm your way back into her life, maybe not. In any case, there's plenty of fish in the sea, and plenty of available women looking for some love and affection.

Reconnecting with Your Kids

Depending on how long you were in the joint, it's more than likely your relationship with your kids has suffered, if only from absence and distance—particularly if you were shipped off far away and received few or no family visits. Your children may harbor considerable resentment of the "How could you do this to me?" variety, which will not be easily overcome. Play it cool, don't force it.

If your wife or ex-wife doesn't want you to see the children when you get out of prison, back off, at least for the short term. She can call your parole officer to complain, quickly get you "violated," and then you're on your way back to prison. A nightmare scenario: You go to your kids' school, and your hostile ex finds out about it and calls the police. A cop picks you up, discovers that you just got out of the joint on parole. He doesn't like convicts, so he calls your parole officer, and the next thing you know, you're in jail. Your wife may not even need to go through the hassle of getting a restraining order from an accommodating criminal justice system. Remember: She's perceived to be the law-abiding citizen and you're always the ex-convict.

The most important relationship you need to establish is with your parole officer. Make sure it's as agreeable as possible. Be courteous and demonstrate that you have a place to live and a decent job. If you've had a couple of monthly visits with your parole officer, who appears to be a reasonable person, this relationship may work to your advantage.

Tell your parole officer you plan to visit your children, especially if your ex-spouse is uncooperative. If and when you meet your ex-wife and children, it's a good idea to take along a respectable member of the community or objective third party, like a minister, priest, or rabbi, who can act as an intermediary or, if necessary, a witness. This may protect you if your former wife makes up stories about your behavior during this visit. It would be ideal if your parole officer came along, but they're overburdened and rarely perform this kind of service.

Bottom line: You need to be incredibly patient negotiating the potentially rough waters. Don't expect your family to welcome you with open arms.

When it comes to getting your kids back, first ask yourself, what's best for them? Would they be better off in their current situation or with you? Be honest, and try to avoid emotional neediness. You can't get back your lost years, you can't start over as if nothing's happened, and you can't just pick up where you left off. It shouldn't be about your needs, but about theirs.

In order to restore custody of your kids (full or joint), you need to get back on your feet again, meaning you need a way to support yourself and a place to live. In some cases, regaining custody of your children may be relatively easy. Why? Because your mother, sister, or aunt are happy to return the little ones (or maybe not so little ones) to you. It'll probably be more difficult to retrieve the kids from the bureaucratic grasp of human service agencies, foster care, or group homes. If your children have been legally adopted by some couple in Alaska, and you live in Florida, you're pretty much out of luck.

If your wife will not permit you to see your children, you'll probably have to hire an attorney to represent you in family court and submit a motion for the return of, joint custody of, or visiting privileges with your kids.

Finding Suitable Employment

Finding a job is a job in itself. A felony conviction will seriously impair your ability to find reasonable work—employers tend to shy away from hiring convicted felons. Most prisoners will lie to the parole board about some possible job they'll get with a friend or relative once they get out. In reality, this so-called job is simply a means of getting the parole board to release you. Or if you do have a job lined up, you might find it really isn't suitable because it's on the other side of town and you don't have transportation to get to it, or it's in another city that you're unwilling or unable to relocate to. Or your brother-in-law or whomever really doesn't need an extra employee—especially an ex-con.

You need to acquire the right set of clothes for your job search. One of the myths about release day is that you'll leave prison with $200 and a new suit. More likely, all you'll get will be a bus ticket and a five dollar bill. You can't go looking for a job wearing your prison uniform or the cheap set of clothing they dressed you out in on the day you were released. The first thing most guys do when they get out of the joint is dump these cheap rags in the garbage or burn them in the back yard as a symbolic gesture to celebrate their freedom. (Be careful in the process not to violate any city ordinances against unlawful lighting of fires or burning of trash!)

Next, pick up the local newspaper, see where the jobs are, travel to them, and fill out job applications. Make sure you fill out the application neatly. When you get to *"Have you ever been arrested for or convicted of a felony?"* write "yes." You have no choice, because when you come to the part about your previous work history, you're going to be unable to explain those wide years-at-a-time gaps in your employment record.

Just do your best without lying on the application, and then ask to speak with the manager or head of human resources or personnel. If you simply leave the application with the secretary or on the counter, you'll never get a call back. Without appearing or acting abusive, don't take no for an answer or leave the business establishment without meeting the boss. When he or she appears, introduce yourself, look him or her in the eye, extend a handshake, and give him or her your application. Wait patiently while he or she looks it over, then ask for an interview. Hopefully, if you've done what we advise and the person has an open mind, you'll receive some attention. Whatever happens, thank the employer for his or her time and consideration.

Also, keep track of the places where you filled out applications, if only for the simple fact that your parole officer is going to want to know if you are actively searching for employment. An especially smart thing to do is photocopy each completed application that you submit. This will help you build a file to demonstrate to your parole officer that you're complying with your parole condition by pursuing a job. This may require you to leave the site and photocopy the application. So be it. You need to accumulate appropriate documentation.

If you do get invited for an interview or manage to speak to the head of personnel, keep your head up, your back straight, and tell the truth with sincerity. Try to pay attention to your language, avoiding convict slang and four-letter words. As with any job, you need to sell yourself and convince the employer to give you a chance, not so much because you need employment, but because you'll be a good employee.

Keeping a Job

When you're hired, remember to report to work on time, do your job, and don't run your mouth off, especially about prison. Try not to make friends with your co-workers, and keep to yourself. Do your job and go home. If you socialize with employees after hours, eventually they're all going to know that you just got out of prison, and the next thing you know you may get fired. Be careful about sharing your convict history, as it may impress some teenagers but upset their parents and your boss. The manager does not want the ex-con to unduly influence the rest of the workers.

You'll also need a W-2 form and steady paycheck to show your parole officer. Avoid seasonal, part-time, or casual employment. In these situations, the boss typically calls you up in the morning and asks you if you want to work that day. Or the job is weather permitting. If conditions outside are bad (rain or snow), you don't work. That's why most construction jobs, outside painting gigs, or roofing jobs are probably inappropriate. Your parole officer wants to see that both the time you work and your pay are consistent. You also don't want to work at a job that only pays cash.

You also don't want to work at any establishment where people are using or selling alcohol or illegal drugs, for example, bars and restaurants with liquor licenses. Quite often, you won't know what's going on behind the scenes in a bar until it's too late. When the heat comes down because of some illegal activity, your managers or co-workers may well hang it on you, the ex-con.

Don't be a patsy or fall guy. We've heard stories of legitimate-sounding businesses that purposely hire ex-cons only to have someone to put the finger on when the place gets busted, like when a car dealership is charged with selling stolen auto parts or a bar is raided for illegal drug sales. You need to work for an established business with a telephone and address, and to report every day so you can be observed working by the parole authorities.

Your parole officer will verify your employment by calling your boss and then, eventually, visiting your work site. You don't want an on-the-road job, like an interstate truck driver or door-to-door salesman. In such situations, the officer will be unable to verify that you're working.

Parole officers are a suspicious lot, and they tend to think (often rightly) that parolees are up to no good and will either go back into "business" (selling dope, burglarizing homes, stealing cars) or will pull some illegal scam on the side. And why not? Some ex-cons want to get back everything they lost while they were doing time. They get some legitimate-looking job with full intentions of reestablishing their place in the illegal marketplace. For example, some former drug dealers come out of prison saying they're going to go straight and work a 9-to-5 job. Maybe they even believe it. Unfortunately, they end up returning to a life of crime. But because they've been out of circulation, they no longer know the lay of the land like they used to—they're out of touch with suppliers and customers. When they do go back into business, they stumble into trouble.

Staying Clean

Although your friends and associates may have escaped the dragnet back when you first took a fall, since then they probably have come under the watchful eyes of the authorities. The bottom line is you need to go straight, because you now have a criminal record. The cops have your photo, fingerprints, address, previous criminal history, and maybe even your DNA. You're a "made man," made in the worst way. You're now one of the Usual Suspects, easily tracked or placed under surveillance, subject to having your parole violated if you're even suspected of being remotely related to crime.

You need to adjust to a more modest, even boring, lifestyle, where you get up in the morning, go to work, stay out of the bars, go to bed early, and live within your means. Apart from that, have fun!

Living Arrangements

The most important thing you need when you get out of prison is a place to live. If you weren't assigned to a halfway house (which is another set of headaches), you'll need to find suitable living arrangements on your own. Let's assume you walk out the gate with no halfway house and go straight to the street. You'll need a bed that night, and may have no money to pay for a motel room. You need to call somebody—for example, your mother or brother—for a couch to sleep on. But this will probably only be a temporary solution.

You don't want to be a roommate with your fast-lane buddies, who party all night and sell drugs on the side. You need a stable situation where you will not be tempted to return to the wild side. You can't live just anywhere, especially not where people keep firearms. This includes your old man's deer rifle or cousin's shotgun. If your parole officer makes a home visit and sees a Civil War musket hanging over the fireplace mantel, you may be busted and sentenced to five years in a federal prison.

It's best to live alone in a quiet neighborhood with a low crime rate and few police. Try to avoid downtown ghettos, barrios, tenderloin districts, or trailer parks; the problem is, you may not be able to afford anything better. Your best bet is to look for a modest apartment or even a room in a middle-class community. Cover your tattoos, watch your language, keep your noise down, try to blend in with the locals, and under no circumstances invite your crook friends over.

The Danger of Owning a Car

A final word to the wise. You don't need to own a car, or if you do to get to work, don't drive around unnecessarily. Most people get arrested when they're stopped in their vehicles. If you must buy a car, try to register it in someone else's name (obviously, you should have all registration and insurance information in the car with you at all times). You especially don't want the license plates in your name. The police will run your tags, discover that you are a parolee, pull over the vehicle, order you out of the car, and maybe even point a gun at your head. You also don't want to drive a jalopy with a broken taillight or no muffler, because that will attract undue attention, especially from the law.

Be careful and modest. If you can, dress straight, drive a late model, and whenever possible, let someone else sit behind the wheel.

The Community Gets What the Community Wants

Ex-cons work minimum-wage, dead-end jobs (as do countless honest citizens, who somehow manage to survive without violating the rights, property, and lives of their fellow members of the community). Cons released on parole or community service fail at an alarming rate—they either escape from custody or are returned to prison.

In the penitentiary, they lived in cages; in the community, they are kept on a short leash. They don't take freedom for granted. They expect to have their parole violated, to be rearrested and returned to prison. With so few resources and prospects, and so much ever-mounting frustration, the results are as inevitable as they are drearily predictable.

Chapter 13

Revolving Doors: Fixing the Incarceration Machine

No matter what the length of the term, doing time in prison is a long, hard ride. This you've probably gathered no matter what stage of your sentence you're in—perhaps the handcuffs have just been placed on your wrists as the judge has rendered his or her sentence, or the jail transport is winding its way through the final stages of the entrance to your new facility, or the last steel door or gate has opened to your freedom in the community, and there is that hesitation when you're not sure whether to shake the guard's hand to say good-bye, or simply move on.

Surviving imprisonment requires patience and humility. Your battle is with time, the months and years that pass as you age behind the wall. Despite the dangers of assault, the struggle is more mental than physical; the real threat is to your sanity. Your mental health is more precious and vulnerable than flesh and bone. You may recover from a beating or stabbing, but never recover the peace of mind robbed by the terror of time.

So, as the time passes, you must keep your head up, take the pain, not give one inch to fear, and fight to maintain your dignity.

Prisoners with the best chance of surviving are those who have prior experience with collective living in close quarters. Men who grew up in orphanages or group homes, lived in university dorms, or served in the military, may have acquired the social skills to live in crowded prison cellblocks.

Obviously, prisoners who've done a previous stretch in jail or prison may have a greater chance of surviving, too. They know the ways of the penitentiary and have already climbed the learning curve. Still, even experienced convicts dread reincarceration, as doing time only gets harder as a man ages. The old con knows he is tired and can no longer bear the noise and nonsense of the young men, the cold of penitentiaries in winter, or the inadequate medical attention when he gets sick. He knows he's on his last legs, and if his sentence is long, or the conditions of confinement severe, he may die in prison.

Shifting Gears

Here's where we get all radical on you. We talk about the massive incarceration blitz since the 1980s, the reasons for this, and how the prison system in the United States might be improved upon or scaled back, making life for everyone in this country—those on the inside and the outside—more tolerable and hopeful.

The War on Drugs

Every year, millions of people are arrested and hundreds of thousands of people sentenced to long prison terms. Most convicts serving time are incarcerated for drug offenses. Many of these persons, with the exception of their use, abuse, or trafficking in illegal substances were, before being imprisoned, law-abiding citizens with no previous criminal record. The crusade against illegal drugs is the engine driving the dramatic increase in federal expenditures on police, courts, and prisons. Drug czars and the respective law enforcement agencies have fought this war in earnest since the beginning of the Reagan administration, through the succeeding two decades of Republican and Democratic presidential administrations.

The war on drugs has lead to the passage of new laws that expand the federal government's ability to conduct search and seizure of homes, cars, boats, businesses, and financial instruments, including funds designated for legal defense. Furthermore, the severe sentencing of convicted drug offenders provides the government with additional means to compel cooperation of defendants and witnesses against their own friends and family. The drug war continues to define citizens as "enemies of the state," persons to be indicted, convicted, and sentenced to spend years in government confinement.

The aggressive criminal justice policies of the past two decades have only resulted in overcrowded prisons with a high rate of recidivism. As noted in Chapter 1, "Busted!" there is an entire nation within a nation in this country, prisons filled with cons, half of whom will return to the joint shortly after release.

Is there anything we can do about the growing prison populations? About the poor living conditions found in many federal and state prisons? About the high recidivism rates? About the lack of appropriate rehabilitation programs? Answers are difficult, but there are possible solutions if we decide to dedicate resources to experiments in rehabilitation and restorative justice.

The Three Rs: Rehabilitation, Reform, and Recidivism

Taxpayers may be surprised to find out that many prison systems have officially repudiated the idea that they're responsible for rehabilitation. Given the growth in prison populations, the reduction in prison programming, and the transformation of prisons into penal warehouses, the idea is no longer seriously considered feasible. Prison administrators have nearly given up on rehabilitation, as they devote their budgets to cement, bricks, and steel to build more facilities to house a growing prisoner population.

Clearly, the lack of rehabilitation programs (like college courses, real vocational training, parenting classes, and psychological therapy and services) contributes to convicts failing parole and returning to prison. In effect, this perpetual incarceration machine is growing because it fails to educate, train, and prepare convicts to make a legal and decent living. While prisoners and taxpayers may see rehabilitation as a means of reducing crime and reforming convicts, prison administrators may not share this view. Wardens appear to have limited their mission to the security and custody problems of their institutions (no escapes and less violence). Unfortunately, the performance evaluations of prisons or prison administrators have rarely been tied to rehabilitation, lowering recidivism, or the relative success of prisoners; and it's hard to measure these outcomes. Prison administrators have passed this problem off to the community. However, if you lock someone up for a couple of years, in all reality you should be able to do something productive with them, right?

The political will to reform prisoners is almost nonexistent. That's why few efforts are ever made to understand why some prisoners go straight when they leave prison and become productive and law-abiding citizens. Thanks to the hard work of a few prison staff, prisoners' own initiative, and time itself, some men and women do "mature out" of crime. In every joint there is a handful of prison staff who come to work every day and attempt to help individual prisoners. They may do this informally through conversation, setting a good example, or operating specific programs. Many of these men and women find satisfaction in helping convicts to grow, learn, and internalize the attitudes and skills needed to live productive, law-abiding lives.

Ultimately, though, if a prisoner wants to reform, more than likely, he or she will have to do most of the hard work on his or her own. This usually requires educating himself or herself through what few courses are available. This also requires reading. After all, books will take you anyplace you have the courage to dream.

Men and women who've been locked up 24 hours a day, seven days a week should be provided a correctional experience that prepares them for successful reintegration back into the community. Correctional officers operate penal facilities that focus almost exclusively on convict management and control. They do little more than control the movement of convicts through the institution, directing them to enter or exit cells, stand in line, or walk through metal detectors.

It's time to rethink how correctional facilities are run. For example, minimum security correctional camps holding cons with short sentences do not need guards and fences. The money spent on these things would be better used on programs rather than security, education instead of cement and steel.

And if we really want to lower recidivism rates, prisoners should be released with Social Security cards, current drivers' licenses, and sufficient gate money to cover rent and food for three months. They should be free of community custody punishment, and provided, upon their request, with professional services (employment assistance, personal and family counseling, drug and alcohol treatment programs, and medical services). We recognize that these ideas are controversial, and some people would consider them to be undeserved privileges for lawbreakers. Still, we think these services will help some ex-prisoners better adjust to the free world, thus reducing the likelihood that they will return to a life of crime.

Federal and state law is replete with repeat offender statutes. The severity of these statutes, as provided by either United States Code or various state codes, that dramatically enhance sentences for career criminals, makes it imperative that the process of prisoner release and reincarceration be addressed. Every year, 500,000 or more prisoners will be released into the community.

Let's Give Restorative Justice a Try

Throughout history, there have always been well-meaning individuals and organizations that have tried to reform prisons and in some cases even abolish them. Quakers, who ironically established one of the very first jails in America (the Walnut Street Jail in Philadelphia), are in the forefront of prison abolition. Among the practices that they advocate is the use of restorative justice as a means to promote reintegration of deviant members back into the community. The process emphasizes group negotiation, the needs of victims, and the responsibility of criminal offenders to accept the consequences for their behavior by paying restitution, doing community service, and encouraging a process of reconciliation based on repentance, apology, and forgiveness.

Not only is this perspective popular among Quakers, it's also supported by a handful of other religious communities because it has a spiritual side, based on reparation of social injuries suffered by both victims and offenders. Restorative justice is experimenting with Victim Offender Reconciliation Programs (inelegantly dubbed VORP), facilitated by trained mediators and sponsored by police and courts that consist of face-to-face encounters between victim and offender in cases that have entered the criminal justice system and the offender has admitted the offense. Even the Clinton Administration, through the U.S. Department of Justice, flirted with the idea of restorative justice.

One of the most radical solutions is to completely eliminate prison. The Abolitionist tradition seeks to limit the use of penal institutions by providing alternatives to incarceration. Although this proposal may appear utopian, it has considerable merit. There are clearly a large number of people serving time for nonviolent offenses who need not be there or who can be better managed in the community.

How Can We Realistically Change Things?

How can we change things? The first step is to change public awareness: People in this country need to know what the prison system in the United States is really like—not how most movies or books present them. Once we know how much they cost and how ineffective they are at rehabilitation, it's likely that more people will push for prison reform. Prisons need to be more open to inspection, investigation, and interviews of prisoners by the media and academic researchers. Hopefully these contacts will document how brutality, corruption, and illegal activities of convicts and prison personnel are commonplace. At the same time they should investigate how idleness, boredom, and the lack of educational opportunities and appropriate vocational training leads to despair, mental illness, and violence. Reporters, in particular, need access to prisons. They also need to be better educated about the conditions of prisoners and the powers of guards and administrators.

Correctional facilities need to have periodic open houses where the public gets to see what actually happens in jails and prisons. Admittedly, not all parts of prison will or should be open to the public. Still, encouraging the free world to see as much as possible about what happens behind the razor wire will help them get a better picture of the concerns of convicts and correctional officers.

Finally, Hollywood movies, newspapers and magazines, and novels often portray sensationalized accounts of prison life. Since most people get their information about prison from these media outlets, it's crucial that they provide more accurate accounts of prison life. These portrayals lead some young men and women to harbor unrealistic notions that going to jail or prison is a rite of passage or an exciting way to pass the time. As this book demonstrates, nothing could be further from the truth. The novelty quickly wears off, while the fear and drudgery remain. Still, more and more Americans are entering jails, and the system is all too willing to accommodate them.

Appendix A

Slammer Slang: A Glossary

7-Up   A warning that a guard is approaching.

10-10   A prisoner who is murdered while incarcerated.

911   An officer is approaching.

AB   Aryan Brotherhood.

ace boon coon   An inmate's best buddy.

ADX   Administrative Max Florence, located in Colorado, the highest-security federal prison in the country. ADX convicts are confined to control units, and there's no general population or controlled movement. The prisoners live and eat in their cells.

air lift   Federal Bureau of Prisons term for transporting prisoners using large commercial-type aircraft, including jets confiscated from major airlines. The prisoners refer to this as "con air."

all day   A life sentence.

American gulag   A convict's perspective that prisoners are incarcerated in the American prison system for social, economic, and political reasons.

attitude adjustment   A drug craving; or physical assault by an officer.

badge   Correctional officer.

banger   Knife, usually homemade. Also called: shank, burner, ox, steel.

bean chute   Food slot in a prison cell door.

beef   Disciplinary charge.

big house   Prison.

big jab   Death by lethal injection.

blanket party   An attacker sneaks up and throws a blanket over the victim's head so that the attacker won't be identified.

blind   Area where a prisoner can't be seen by a guard.

blues   Prison-issue clothes.

boat   To be transferred out of prison or to another prison.

bone crusher   Very large shank or knife.

boof   Contraband stowed in the anus. Also known as: hoop, keester, pack.

boot camp   Alternative incarceration that resembles military training and may shorten sentence.

booty check   Anal search for contraband.

border brothers   Mexican inmates.

boss   A guard or correctional officer, especially in the American South or Canada.

BP Process   Federal Bureau of Prisons "Administrative Remedy Process" for prisoners to file complaints, as a prerequisite for filing legal briefs in federal court.

brake fluid   Mind-control medication, like liquid Thorazine, which is used like chemical restraints to manage prison populations.

Buck Rogers time   An extremely long prison term where the parole seems to be pushed out forever.

bug   An insane person. Usually accused of buggin'.

bulldog   An intimidating, domineering prisoner.

bullet   One-year prison term.

bum rap   An erroneous conviction.

bumpin ya gums   Refers to when someone is talking too much.

bunkie   Cellmate.

burnt up   To receive disciplinary action.

butched in   Forced to perform oral sex.

call out sheet   FBOP official memo posted in housing units to alert prisoners and staff where convicts need to report the next day. Call out sheets list cell changes, new work assignments, visits, meetings with case managers or other staff.

cap   The amount of pot that fits into a chopstick cap.

catcher   Sexually submissive prisoner.

catnap   Short prison term.

C.C.   Consecutive prison sentences.

chalking   To distract guards while another prison breaks a rule.

chasing the dragon   An addict searching for heroin.

cheese eater   An informer, or rat.

chester   Child molester. Also known as short eyes, diaper sniper.

click up   To join a gang.

commissary   Prison store that sells basic food items, smokes, clothing, stamps, paper, and toiletries.

connet   A female convict.

contraband   Anything on your person or found in your cell or housing area that is unauthorized, meaning not sold in commissary or on your official property list. These items are confiscated and destroyed by staff. Being caught with contraband may result in an incident report (a shot), which could get you an immediate trip to the hole, loss of good time, or transferred to a higher-security institution.

controlled movement   Convicts may only move from one location to another on the hour. They are required to have staff permission to exit or enter each location, and are monitored by officers through a series of security doors and perimeters. Most medium and maximum security facilities have rigid regulations restricting the controlled movement of the general population.

control unit   High-security housing units in disciplinary prisons—for example, ADX Florence and USP Marion.

cop out   Formal request by prisoner or staff for cell or work reassignment, transfer to another prison, adding a new person to a visiting list, a medical appointment, request for BP forms (for administrative remedy), or official report on days left to serve on sentence.

corner   A group of prisoners who hang out together, not necessarily in a gang.

count   Head count of convicts, which takes place several times a day. *La cuenta* in Spanish.

crate   A carton of cigarettes. Also known as a brick.

crime of passion   Sex offender.

daddy   Dominant partner of a homosexual relationship. Usually a protector.

DCer   A federal prisoner who comes from the Washington, D.C., area, including Maryland or Virginia. Usually used to refer to African-Americans convicted of street crimes in the D.C. metro area.

deuce   A short, two-year sentence.

diesel therapy   Riding around in prison transport for days, weeks, or months.

dime   Ten-year sentence.

ding wing   Ward for the criminally insane.

direct order   Oral command issued by an officer. There is no such thing as an indirect order in prison.

dis   Abbreviation for disrespect.

disturbance   Low-intensity violence, destruction of property, or vandalism inside the prison.

dog food   Heroin.

donkey dick   Sliced meat.

doo rag   Scarf or bandanna worn around an inmate's head.

dope fiend move   Dishonest move.

down letter   A letter stating that parole has been denied.

dragon's tongue   Overcooked corned beef with the consistency of leather.

dressed out   To be covered with urine or feces thrown by a prisoner.

drop a dime   To rat someone out.

ducat   Internal prison passes.

duck   A guard who informs or gossips to the prisoners about other guards.

dump truck   Lawyer who plea-bargains at the expense of the prisoner.

ear hustling   Eavesdropping.

eight ball   Eight-year prison term.

electronic jacket   Computer records kept by the government on individuals. All cons and ex-cons have electronic jackets.

eyeball   When a prisoner tries to stare down a guard.

family style   Sodomy in the missionary position.

FBOP   Federal Bureau of Prisons.

FCI   Federal Correctional Institution, a medium security prison.

featherwood   A white man's wife or girlfriend.

federal prison jacket   The Central Inmate File that includes all of a prisoner's records.

felon fodder   Inmates.

fifi   Artificial vagina; sex toy.

fish   New prisoners who have just entered the system.

fish line   Devised by prisoners to transport items from one cell to another.

fish tank—A holding cell in a jail or prison where they house fish, sometimes called a drunk tank or bullpen in county jails.

flavor   Factory-manufactured cigarette.

flip flop   To change places during sodomy.

flip the pad   To flip over a bunk mattress.

FMC   Federal Medical Center, a minimum or medium security prison for prisoners with chronic or acute medical conditions.

foo-foo   To wear deodorant, aftershave, or cologne.

four minute job   Shower.

FPC   Federal Prison Camp, for nonviolent offenders serving fewer than 10 years.

free pass   To be let off the hook by a guard.

free world   The world beyond the prison wall or fence, where free people live.

FTC   Federal Transport Center, a medium security facility where prisoners are routed by car, bus, and plane to other institutions.

fug   Cigarette.

furlough   Some prison systems authorize minimum security prisoners who are within one year of release to go home a few days to see family and attempt to arrange future housing and employment.

galboy   Passive partner in a homosexual relationship.

gang bangers   Gang members.

gangster   Name for HIV.

gas house   Prison public lavatory.

gated out   Released from prison.

general population   Prisoners who are not in segregation, protective custody, or medical units.

get hit   To have a prison sentence extended.

getting short   Prisoners with less than one year to do (time to serve) before their release. These men and women are generally quiet and attempt to disengage from the convict culture as they prepare for re-entry. In prison it's considered rude by both prisoners and staff to mess with these cons, as it may create delays in their release.

gladiator fight   A fight between two prisoners staged for the entertainment of the other prisoners and guards.

good time   Prisoners may receive time off their sentences for good behavior. This is calculated differently in each prison system. Some convicts may call this "sweet time," as it refers to time you will not have to serve inside, but will do on the street when released to parole.

greenlight   To be marked for death by other prisoners.

gumbie   A male transvestite or transgendered person in prison.

gunned down   To be covered in urine or feces by another prisoner.

hack   A disparaging term referring to a correctional officer.

halfway house   A community program residence or work release center where prisoners are assigned upon leaving prison. Usually the convicts are required to pay for room and board, keep a job, and follow strict rules.

hard time   A long, hard sentence, usually refers to prisoners who refuse to play by the rules, hence they are often disciplinary problems.

heart check   A dangerous act, such as murder, performed by a prisoner to prove loyalty to a gang.

herb   A passive prisoner.

high class   To describe someone who has hepatitis C.

hit a lick   Masturbate.

hog   A prisoner who refuses to back down from a fight.

hole   Where a prisoner is placed if he or she has violated the institutional rules or is unable to live safely in general population. Also called segregation, protective custody, administrative segregation, segregated housing unit, detention, disciplinary detention, or control unit.

homes   Affectionate abbreviation for homeboy.

hook-up   When a guard lies to get a prisoner in trouble.

hot rail   A group of prisoners surrounding a couple having sex so that others can't see.

house   A prisoner's cell.

house arrest   Instead of being sentenced to prison, a person is given an electronic monitoring device or phone tether, usually an ankle bracelet, and required to serve time at home. This allows the prisoner to go to work, support his or her family, and care for children. If the prisoner violates the correctional contract or agreement, he or she may be sent to prison to serve the sentence.

hung up   When a prisoner hangs himself.

illing   To describe crazy behavior of another inmate.

ink   Tattoo.

inmate   A pejorative term used by prison staff referring to their captive population. Convicts rarely use this term. Thus we have avoided its use in this book except when it's used as an official designation.

inmate central file   This is a large file that includes prisoners' PSI report, FBI and police records, rap sheet, and prison records, including reports from medical staff, work supervisors, program staff, and correctional officers. It may contain a con's entire prison record, for example documenting transfers to different prisons, cell and work assignments, telephone and visiting lists, commissary balances, incident reports, and program participation.

iron pile   Exercise weights.

issue   The crime the prisoner was convicted of.

jacket   Labeled as an informant.

jailhouse lawyer   A prisoner with at least a working knowledge of the law who helps other inmates file legal actions.

jeff   Horse around, have fun with someone.

jody   Cuckolded male prisoner.

joe   Cigarette.

joint mentality   The perspective prisoners acquire from living in a total institution, where every aspect of their life is regimented and regulated.

jones   Drug addiction or other craving.

juice card   Favors handed out by guards.

june bug   Submissive prisoner used by others.

kicking it   The act of having sex.

kill zone   The prohibited area next to an outside wall or fence.

kit   Drug paraphernalia.

kitty kitty   A term used by prisoners to refer to female correctional officers.

K-9   Canine police unit.

L   Life sentence.

lady hacks   A term used by prisoners to refer to female correctional officers.

laying the track   Having sex with another prisoner.

lettuce   Prisoner term for a group of inmates involved in a gang raping.

lifer   Someone who is doing a life sentence. A prisoner may be sentenced to life without parole, which means they'll die in prison, or 25 years to life. Generally, any sentence over 25 years is considered a life sentence, even if it may be commuted by legal authority or parole release. Elderly or medical convicts may consider a much shorter time to be a life sentence. In general, a lifer is expected to die in prison.

limbo   Prisoner term for jail time served before a conviction.

lockdown   When prisoners are confined to their cells during a crisis.

locker banger   A prisoner who breaks into convicts' lockers and steals property.

lockup unit   Detention.

lugged   Handcuffed.

ma   A girlfriend who stands by her man.

mafias   Dark sunglasses.

make paper   Parole.

main line   A federal penitentiary or general population chow hall line. The guards will talk about "standing main line" as they supervise the dining hall in a maximum security prison.

max out   A prisoner serving a life sentence all the way through. A lifer.

MCC   Metropolitan Correction Center, administrative prisons in urban areas, usually high-rises that resemble corporate offices. They may include courtrooms, helicopter pads, and cellblocks or dormitories on many floors. Prisoners move by elevators from housing units to different locations in the facilities, including the "yard," which may be on the roof.

MCFP   Medical Center Federal Prison, the Springfield, Missouri, maximum security prison that includes medical services for seriously ill prisoners. This is where penitentiary convicts receive medical attention.

merry-go-round   A term used on Federal Bureau of Prisons "call out sheet," referring to the process a prisoner goes through their very last day in prison. The convict is provided an official form that requires a number of staff signatures. The prisoner must then visit different locations in the prison where staff sign off. The point is to settle all accounts and alert staff to the scheduled release of the prisoner the next day.

missive   Letter or note written by a prisoner.

monkey   Correctional officer.

moe   A homosexual prisoner who is married.

monster   HIV virus.

MR   Mandatory release at the completion of a prison sentence. The convict goes home with no halfway house or parole time to serve.

mule   Someone, not necessarily another prisoner, who smuggles contraband to an inmate.

nickel   Five-year sentence.

nut up   To go crazy, out of control.

old lady   Submissive partner in a homosexual relationship.

old timer   An inmate who has been incarcerated for a long time.

on his leg   Begging for special privileges.

on pipe   Submissive partner in a male homosexual relationship.

pack   Concealing a weapon.

paper   Proof that another prisoner is a squealer.

paper man   A model prisoner on parole who is only required to mail in a monthly form providing information about residence and employment, and is not required to report on a regular basis to the parole office. They are still subject to the same rules of parole, including unannounced "home visits" by parole authorities and substance abuse testing.

PC Protective custody.

pecker palace Conjugal visiting area.

peckerwood A white person. Known as wood for short.

peel Orange prison issue.

perpetual incarceration machine A criminal justice system that recycles the same people from prison to parole and back to prison.

phone Clearing out the bathroom for private conferences between prisoners.

pig Correctional officer.

pile Exercise weights. Short for iron pile.

pinner Tiny marijuana cigarette.

pitcher Sexually dominant partner in a homosexual relationship.

pole smoker Male homosexual.

prior Previous incarcerations.

prize of the poor Death penalty.

program The prison sentence.

pruno Homemade brew made from fermented fruit.

PSI The pre-sentence investigation prepared for the court by a probation or parole officer. The report summarizes a person's criminal case and concludes with sentencing recommendations. It usually contains a lengthy narration describing the defendants' family, education, work, behavioral, and criminal history. This report is used by the judge to suggest sentencing options, by prison authorities to determine classification and security level, and later by parole board authorities to guide them in their deliberations.

pulling a train Serving consecutive sentences.

pumpkin head A prisoner who has been beaten with an object encased in a pillowcase, whose face is so bruised it resembles a pumpkin.

punks and sissies Homosexuals or prisoners who have been turned out are considered to be punks. Many of these men have

suffered terrible abuse and may be unstable and extremely dangerous. As they mature in the penitentiary, they may become predators
or seek revenge against those who used them sexually.

put grass under you   To walk away from a conversation.

quiet cell   Soundproof cell used for solitary confinement.

rag   Bandana or head scarf.

range-runners or detail crew   Common terms for convicts who
work in housing units where they clean floors and take out the
garbage. They may also be responsible for providing their fellow
prisoners with fresh clothes, bedding, and towels. They usually
sleep all day and do their duties at night while the other men are
locked in their cells.

rat   Someone who provides the guards information about the mis-
behavior of other convicts, expecting something in return; another
name for a snitch.

R.B.   Short for Rich Bitch, or a prisoner who owns a lot of stuff.

real friend   Someone from the outside who sends care packages,
including money.

reception or diagnostic center   The entrance to many state
prison systems, where prisoners are first confined while they are
evaluated before being transferred on to minimum, medium, or
maximum security institutions. They may return here when being
processed for release and re-entry to the community.

R-and-D   FBOP term for receiving and departure. This is usually
a secure location within the prison where prisoners arrive or leave
the institution. It is a large room where all convicts are processed
at one time, including having their personal property catalogued,
being strip-searched, "dressed out" in uniforms or street clothes,
fingerprinted, and mug shot.

re-entry   Refers to the process of leaving prison to re-enter the
free community.

retired   A prisoner with a life sentence without parole.

rev Religious prisoner.

riding leg Brown-nosing for special privileges.

road kill Cigarettes made from the tobacco of butts, usually picked up on the side of the road while on a chain gang.

rolling gulag Prison transports.

rughead Derogatory term for a black prisoner.

running someone's tags Getting information on another inmate.

safe A female prisoner's vagina is referred to as this when she stows contraband there.

schooled Well versed in prison life.

scooper Spoon.

screw A disparaging term referring to a guard or correctional officer.

segregation Another name for the hole.

shakedown Cell search by a correctional officer.

shank Convict weapon fashioned out of wood, metal, plastic, or glass, and used to cut or stab. These may be made out of nearly anything, including toothbrushes, combs or hairbrushes, windowpanes, or building materials.

shit The HIV virus.

shive A shank, or knife.

short line The mess hall line for off-duty convict kitchen staff. It may also refer to special dietary meals, for example, those prisoners authorized to be served kosher food or required by medical conditions to have special diets (no sugar or low salt). Usually the line is shorter and the food better than on the main line.

shot Incidence or disciplinary report. An officer will write a shot, or write up, a prisoner for violating prison rules. There are ascending levels of shots going from minor to serious infractions, with the worst resulting in criminal charges, for example, assault on an officer or another prisoner.

shower hawk   Someone who stalks showers for victims.

signed in   Request protective custody.

skeet   Heroin.

slam down   To be placed in solitary confinement.

sleeved   An arm completely covered in tattoos.

sliming   Throwing human waste at a hack.

slow-playing   Complying with direct orders very slowly, as a means of resistance.

snitch   A prisoner who informs on other convicts and expects special privileges in return from staff.

spun out   Out of control, idiotic.

square   Cigarette.

state issue   What is given to inmates as part of their prison issues, such as their clothes.

strap up   To get a shank.

street   Life beyond the prison walls. Also know as the World.

stun belt   A disabling or disciplining device strapped around a prisoner's waist that emits an electrical shock if the individual is perceived to be a danger or disruptive.

supermax   A disciplinary penitentiary where convicts are held in control unit single cells 23 to 24 hours a day. These prisons have no dining hall, vocational or educational programs, or recreation facilities.

tailor made   A factory manufactured cigarette.

tat   Short for tattoo.

team   FBOP term referring to Unit Manager, Work Supervisor, Correctional Counselor, and Case Manager. Depending upon the security level of the prisoner, and time left to be served by the prisoner, the convict will go to team every 90 days, 180 days, or once a year. The prisoner's institutional program will be reviewed by the team, inmate requests considered, and deliberations made about program changes.

thorazine shuffle The gait of prisoners who are so whacked out (drugged up) on psychotropic medication they can barely lift their feet when they walk—instead they appear to glide or moon-dance down the corridor. They may also have difficulty speaking coherent sentences.

tit Illegal drugs.

T-Jones Prisoner's parents.

tossing a cell The common practice of searching a prisoner's cell for contraband, usually performed by a group of hacks.

tuned-up When groups of guards beat up a prisoner, usually while he is in restraints. The correctional officers do this to teach the convict that they are the boss, exercise revenge, and disable prisoners who resist their authority. Usually this happens after a convict refuses a direct order or assaults staff. The beating happens in a remote section of the prison, like an empty hallway or segregation cell.

turned out Used to describe a straight male who is used for homosexual sex, as in "he's been turned out."

turnkey An archaic name for jailer, it refers to how guards are required to turn a key to mark the time on a device affixed to a cellblock wall, as they make their rounds. It can also refer to their principle activity, which is turning keys in locks.

USP United States Penitentiary, a main line maximum security prison.

walking down paper The process of serving the balance of an original sentence on parole.

waterhead A prisoner others consider stupid, or who does stupid things.

went up in that fire A euphemism for an AIDS victim.

wood   Short for peckerwood, a derogatory term for a white person.

world   Life beyond the prison walls. Also known as the Street.

write up   Report of disciplinary action.

yard   Prison yard used for exercise.

yellow brick road   The yellow border painted on the yard that the prisoner must stay within.

yolked   Describing a muscular prisoner.

Appendix B

We Understand, Son: Prison Reform Advocacy Groups

There are many groups working locally, nationally, and internationally to reform prisons and help prisoners or ex-cons. Some of the international or national organizations have state or local chapters, which you may find listed in your local telephone directory or on the World Wide Web. Most of these groups are non-profit organizations that welcome volunteers.

American Civil Liberties Union (ACLU) National Prison Project

Branch of the national ACLU that works on prison legal issues. They don't handle individual cases, but only litigate large-scale state or national prison reform legal actions, such as prison rights or medical issues. Contact: 1875 Connecticut Ave. N.W., Suite 410, Washington, D.C. 20009, phone: 202-234-4830.

Amnesty International

Amnesty International, which typically is concerned with the torture of individuals, is now involved with monitoring prison conditions in the United States. They also published a report about the inhumanity of using stun belts in prisons and courtrooms. Contact: Amnesty International, International Secretariat, 1 Easton Street, London, WC1X 8DJ, UK.

Center for Rational Correctional Policy

Web site with considerable information on the criminal justice system, including links to many state departments of corrections websites, governmental agencies, non-governmental agencies, and the death penalty. Website: www.pierce.simplenet.com/prisonerresources.html.

The Center on Juvenile and Criminal Justice

A private non-profit organization whose mission is to "reduce society's reliance on the use of incarceration as a solution to social problems." Main Administrative Office 1622 Folsom Street, San Francisco, CA 94103, phone 415-621-5661, fax 415-621-5466; D.C. Office: 1234 Massachusetts Ave, NW, Suite C1009 Washington, D.C. 20005, phone: 202-737-7270 fax: 202-737-7271, www.cjcj.org/contact.html.

Centurion Ministries

Assists in the exoneration of wrongfully convicted persons in U.S. prisons. Contact: James McCloskey, Centurion Ministries Inc., 32 Nassau St., 3rd Floor, Princeton, NJ 08542, phone: 609-921-0334.

Committee to Free the Innocent

Advocacy organization based in the nation's capital. 1627 K Street, 12th Floor, Washington, D.C. 20006.

Critical Resistance

Left liberal organization whose membership includes activists such as Angela Davis. Holds periodic conferences on the problems of the prison system in the United States. Contact: Box 339, Berkeley, CA 94701, phone: 510-643-2094, fax: 510-845-8816, e-mail: critresist@aol.com.

FCNetwork

Provides information on children of prisoners, parenting programs for prisoners, prison visiting, incarcerated fathers and mothers, hospitality programs, and prison marriage. The website is sponsored by Family and Corrections Network (FCN), publisher of FCN REPORT, said to be the only national publication devoted to families of offenders. Contact FCN's 32 Oak Grove Road, Palmyra, VA 22963, phone: 804-589-3036, fax: 804-589-6520, e-mail: fcn@fcnetwork.org.

Human Rights Watch

A well-known international nongovernmental organization supported by contributions from private individuals and foundations to protect the human rights of individuals throughout the world. 350 Fifth Avenue, 34th floor, New York, NY 10118-3299, phone: 212-290-4700, fax: 212-736-1300, e-mail: hrwnyc@hrw.org.

Innocence Project

Provides legal assistance only in cases where prisoners are challenging their convictions based on DNA testing of evidence. Law students work on projects and are supervised by experienced attorneys. Contact: Innocence Project, Benjamin N. Cardozo School of Law, 55 5th Ave., 11th Floor, New York, NY 10003, phone: 212-790-0368.

Journal of Prisoners on Prison

A forum for the publication of academic research, personal experiences, and commentaries on prisons written by convicts, ex-convicts, and scholars. Website: www.cspi.org/books/p/prisoners.htm.

League for Lesbian and Gay Prisoners

Project of the Gay Community Social Services. Contact: 1202 East Pike St., Suite 1044, Seattle, WA, 98122.

National Lawyers Guild

Assists jailhouse lawyers. Contact: Prison Law Project, c/o National Lawyers Guild, 558 Capp Street, San Francisco, CA 94110.

Northwestern University Center for Wrongful Conviction

Initial requests will be reviewed by the Journalism Department and then forwarded to the law students if the matter warrants a full investigation. Contact: Northwestern University Legal Clinic,

Attention: Larry Marshall, 350 E Superior, Room MC-282, Chicago, IL 60611, phone: 312-503-8576, fax: 312-503-8977.

Open Incorporated

A nonprofit organization devoted to producing and marketing educational products for prisoners and ex-cons. P.O. 47223, Garland, TX 75047-2223, phone: 972-271-1971, e-mail: info@openincorporated.org, website: www.openinc.org.

Open Society Institute, Criminal Justice Initiative

Part of the Soros Foundation, which provides grants for programs and research. Committed to "reducing the excessive reliance on punishment and incarceration in the United States, and to promoting fair and equal treatment in all aspects of the U.S. criminal justice system." 400 West 59th St., 3rd Floor, New York, NY 10909, phone: 212-548-0135, website: www.soros.org/crime/contact.htm.

Organization for Sensible and Effective Prison Policy

A resource for prison issues, including wrongful convictions. E-mail: osepp@amandla.org.

Pennsylvania Prison Society

Provides support for Pennsylvania prisoners and their families. Contact: 3 North 2nd St., Philadelphia, PA 19106.

People Organized to Stop Rape of Prisoners

Support and Information for Rape Survivors. Contact: Box 632, Ft. Bragg, CA 95437.

Prison Activist Resource Center

P.O. Box 339, Berkeley, CA 94701.

Prison Law Page

Web page that may be a useful source for information on California Prison Law: www.wco.com/~aerick.

Prisoner Visitation and Support

PVS trains and coordinates "high-quality" citizens to visit with Federal and Military prisoners. They visit inside all maximum and medium security federal prisons, medical prisons, and women's prisons across the United States. 1501 Cherry Street, Philadelphia, PA 19102, phone: 215-241-7117.

Project for Older Prisoners (POPS)

A good source if you are interested in the graying of the prison population. Contact: c/o Jonathan Turley—Director, The National Law Center, 2000 H Street NW, Washington, DC 20006.

The Sentencing Project

Organization that "promotes decreased reliance on incarceration and increased use of more effective and humane alternatives." Excellent source of criminal justice policy analysis, data, and program information. Contact: 514 10th Street, NW Suite 1000 Washington, D.C. 20004, phone: 202-628-0871, fax: 202-628-1091, e-mail: staff@sentencingproject.org, website: www.sentencingproject.org.

Truth in Justice

Another website that discusses wrongful convictions and miscarriages of justice: www.truthinjustice.org/index.htm.

Index